God Unwrapped

God is Love...
but not the kind you're used to

by
Michelle Hollomon

Scripture quotations marked (NIV) are taken from *The Holy Bible: New International Version®* NIV®. Copyright © 1973, 1978, 1984 by International Bible Society. Used by permission of Zondervan Publishing House. Used by permission.

Scripture quotations marked (MSG) are taken from *The Message: New Testament with Psalms and Proverbs*, copyright © 1993, 1994, 1995 by Eugene H. Peterson, published by NavPress, P.O. Box 35001, Colorado Springs, Colorado 80935. Used by permission.

Scripture quotations marked (NAS) are taken from the *New American Standard Bible*. Copyright © The Lockman Foundation 1960, 1962, 1963, 1968, 1971, 1972, 1973, 1975, 1977. Used by permission.

Scripture quotations marked (NKJV) are taken from *The New King James Version*. Copyright © 1979, 1980, 1982, Thomas Nelson, Inc. Used by permission.

Scripture quotations marked (NLT) are taken from the *Holy Bible, New Living Translation* copyright© 1996, 2004, 2007 by Tyndale House Foundation. Used by permission of Tyndale House Publishers Inc., Carol Stream, Illinois 60188. All rights reserved.

Scripture quotations marked (NCV) are taken from *The Everyday Bible: New Century Version*. Copyright © 2002 by Thomas Nelson, Inc. Used by permission.

ISBN: 978-1-60683-352-0

14 13 12 11 10 9 8 7 6 5 4 3 2 1

8201 164th Ave NE, Suite 200
Redmond, WA 98052
michelle@counselingtheeastside.com

Published by Harrison House, LLC
Tulsa, Oklahoma

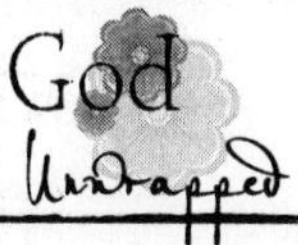

table of contents

Praise for God Unwrapped

Michelle is the real deal! This book is full of grace, but refuses to lean on clichés to address deep heartfelt needs. Michelle is a therapist who combines an excellent understanding of Scripture and of people to develop an insightful book.

God Unwrapped is a great book for those who have been burned by religion, those who have never given Christianity a serious look or those who are looking to take their next right step in their faith but are not sure how.

Ben Sigman, Pastor
Timberlake Christian Church
Redmond, Washington

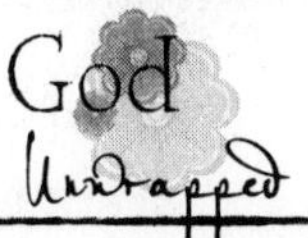

Dedication

This book is dedicated to my amazing children Addison and Evelyn, who show me the face of God every day. Thank you to my family, who has supported me, tolerated me, challenged me, fertilized me and loved me. Thank you Brian for not falling asleep through all the hours I talked about "the book," for the relentless support, and for being the man of my dreams. Thank you to Carolyn who first immersed me in the fountain of God's grace that I've been playing in ever since. Thank you to Joanna, my friend, my sister, my mildred, and Claudine, my co-conspirator. Thank you to my handler and promoter, Jen E. Thank you to Mick for first throwing the dog a bone, to Ed, who added to my repertoire of spiritual father figures and who shaped the outline, and for Amy who gave me hope that it may be worth a read. Thank you to Troy who is always willing to help a sister out. Thank you to the Harrison House team: Chris, Julie, Christina and Lisa, whose professionalism and teamwork I admire. Thank you to Andrew Boyer, videographer extraordinaire. Thank you to the Lydias who reminded me I was going to be ok. Thank you to the Northwest Christian Writers Association who mourn with the mourners and celebrate with the victors. There would be no book, or happiness in my life, for that matter, without the above people. Thank you to Jesus who has anchored me in such an abundant life, and allows me the freedom to explore it.

Note from the Author

Throughout this book, I have used stories and examples designed to help the reader better understand the processes of healing and Christian transformation. The stories are composites and the names, genders, professions, and distinguishing details have all been changed to protect the identities of my previous, current, and imaginary clients.

one

God Isn't Who You Think He Is

"Who among the gods is like you, O Lord?

Exodus 15:11-13 NIV

It had been 6 years and two children since I'd gone SCUBA diving, and I knew from the raised eyebrow of the dive master that I should have taken a refresher course before signing up for the coral reef. Sensing my inexperience, she spent the boat ride to our dive destination shouting crash-course instructions over the noise of the engine. I kept thinking to myself, *it's just like riding a bike—it will come back to me.* After sinking 25 feet below the surface, I discovered that it wasn't just like riding a bike. I couldn't remember what button deflated my jacket, and what button inflated my jacket. No big deal really. All I had to do was calmly pump one button and see if I floated up or down. But "calmly" wasn't something I could master at the moment.

Panic took over instantly and my only thought was, *If I push the wrong button, I will sink, drown and die!* That wasn't really true, but seemed rational enough at the time. I flailed

my arms to the dive master, with wild eyes, and signaled to go up. She signaled confusion. Since I didn't know SCUBA sign for "I'm freaking out," I signaled with my thumb the *strong* desire to go back up. She took hold of my jacket and pumped it a few times until my buoyancy was stabilized, and slowly signaled with her hands for me to calm myself down. She waited about a minute and then with an extraordinary gesture of kindness, she held out her hand so we could dive together.

I completely expected that after reacting the way I did, she would escort me back to the surface, chastise my foolishness, and terminate my dive with a "Hmph!" Instead, she held my hand and gave me the security I needed until I could do it on my own. With only the sounds of bubbles and breath, we swam together as she pointed out the things she wanted me to see. Like the activity backstage of a play, I was amazed by the colors and creatures and coral alive with anemone, hidden by the curtain of water. After we surfaced, she told me that she just couldn't let me leave the reef without experiencing it first. She didn't know me, or owe me anything. But she stepped into my past to reclaim a lost picture of God—a God who wanted me to know and enjoy Him without the fear of falling short—a God who didn't cut me off for my mistakes but helped me overcome them in grace. God used that experience, among many others to replace the distorted ideas of who I thought He was.

Why did I think my dive master would be disappointed in me? Why did I care? Furthermore, why did I panic to the point of not thinking clearly? Why was I surprised by her outstretched hand? Why do people question God's infinite

love and care? Why do people doubt Him when He's done nothing to earn their distrust?

Various misconceptions about God are closely linked to the god-figures in our lives: our parents, coaches, older siblings, bosses, teachers and pastors. We understand God based on what we already know. We formulate who the Heavenly Father is and who we are, because of our childhood experiences. Our authority figures while growing up leave the most influential mark of who we understand God to be. We were parented and groomed by imperfect people, and have automatic assumptions of an imperfect God.

We need a bold new approach to know Him.

God Wikipedia

My husband's mother passed away before our children were born, and I feel like a Wikipedia entry when I tell them about her. You can search *Mexico's Coral Reef* and find out a lot of information, but if you haven't experienced it, you don't know just how incredible it is. So how do I describe Betty Jean Hollomon so they can really grasp the essence of who she was? I describe her attributes. I show them pictures of her. I show them the china pattern that she chose for her wedding registry. When my husband sees them have an interest in science, he mentions his own mother's career and encourages them. Someday, I will let them read the journal she kept when she fought the cancer that took her life. Though I do all I know to describe her, they will not know her this side of heaven.

In the same way, we have many ways of knowing God. We have our own Wikipedia entry named "God" loaded and listed with informative facts. Somebody somewhere uploaded that information, but what kind of "experts" were they? A woman raised in a relationally cold family with little talking or feeling describes feeling distant from God as an adult. A man raised by his mother with no father figure has difficulty seeing God as an involved and attentive Father. A person with hard-to-please parents projects the same assumptions on God, and ends up working hard to measure up. A woman abused by her mother's boyfriend sees God as impotent and unwilling to help.

What if we could think differently? What if we challenged these assumptions and opened up to something better? To really know God, we must make some room for things we don't understand just yet—we must click out of the Wikipedia description of *coral reef* and fly to Cozumel for a dive.

Questions for Self Reflection:

- What kind of god-figures did you have growing up?
- How did they inform your opinion of God?
- How did you learn to see yourself?
- What kind of religious experiences informed your view of God?

Intention Statement:

I will see God in spirit and in truth, and will see myself as He sees me.

Extra Study:

Job 11:7-8; Deuteronomy 4:29; Luke 19:11-27

God
Unwrapped

two

Seeing the Same Old God in a Brand New Way

"Taste and see that the LORD is good. Oh, the joys of those who take refuge in him!"

Psalm 34:8 NLT

"My life wasn't supposed to be like this. It's been one disappointment after another. I'm completely alone, and it's suffocating."

Charlotte bemoaned her life in my office as tears streamed down her face. She was a bright, articulate ballet dancer who taught and performed in a prestigious dance company. She was lovely in every way, inside and out. But years of internalizing pain and negativity had catapulted her into some really bad choices. She was dating a man who threatened her with a knife on more than one occasion. She turned down a well-deserved part because she thought herself unworthy. And she felt utterly alone in the world. Honored with prestige and status for her artistic talent, Charlotte felt increasingly insecure and phony when she danced. Her depression seemed bottomless.

On this appointment, however, after dumping her usual load of anguish, Charlotte said something that surprised me. “Sometimes I sense that something is present with me, something good.” Her sad eyes brightened a little as she spoke the words.

Sensing hope for the first time in a long time, and trying not to seem too eager, I seized the moment, “What do you mean?”

“I don’t know, like a presence, or something.”

“When you encounter this *presence,* how do you feel?”

“I come out of the black hole of my life—just for a moment—and feel the light on my face.”

Suddenly hopeful that we might have some leverage for making progress, I asked, “When do these moments of light happen?”

Charlotte’s eyes drifted to the window and her puffy face glistened in the sunlight. “They start whenever I think that there might be something better out there. That’s when I notice special things around me that make me feel hopeful, like an intricate spider web or a hummingbird or dust particles dancing in the light. That’s when I’m aware of a

presence that knows I need to see good things no matter how small they are."

I floated a possibility by her. "Charlotte, do you think this *something*, this *presence* may have a personal interest in you?"

After a moment of thought she slowly nodded. She spoke about a time she was driving to see her parents. She was afraid of what she knew awaited her at home. As a child, she had been the target of her parents' disapproval, hostility, and belittling. Every time Charlotte went home, she was again immersed in her parents' disappointment toward her.

"On my trip home," she recalled, "I was captivated by the colors and dimensions of the sky and by the dew sparkling on the crops. It all looked so extraordinary and beautiful, I just knew that there was something good out there and I was going to be ok."

Charlotte's experience had convinced her that something good existed outside her dark world. But she wasn't ready to call this something "God" because she didn't see God as good. On occasion, she expressed her desire to have a faith, but whenever she "tried" to believe in God, she ended up feeling guilty. To her, God was just like her parents: a distant, disapproving force who was difficult to please and reluctant to help. When Charlotte was a child, God and religion were used to shame her into better behavior. She was afraid that the toxic religion of her childhood would spoil her new experiences with the goodness she was discovering. I bit my tongue until it hurt, waiting for her discoveries to lead her to the God that I knew.

Like Charlotte, our view of God is closely linked to how the god-figures treated us from early childhood on. Psychologists and attachment theorists and authors of *God Attachment*, Tim Clinton and Joshua Straub write, "Our spiritual journeys are linked to core relational beliefs established early in life based on how we've learned to perceive ourselves and others in our closest relationships."[1] No matter how much we *learn* about God from nature, music, science, art, and the Bible, what we *believe* about Him is strongly shaped by the beliefs and behavior of our original god-figures.

Charlotte has a lot of company in her distorted view of God's goodness, even among Christians. We all find it difficult to believe that God is good all the time because our parents, as good as they may have been, were not good all the time. For example, you may think that God wants more than you can give because your dad was strict and demanding. Or perhaps your mom always leaned on you for help but wasn't much interested in helping you, so you think of God as a taker more than a giver. If you grew up feeling neglected, shamed, or used by those responsible for your care and nurture, you likely suspect the same flaws in God.

What you believe about God and yourself is indispensable to your growth and success at every level. Your view of God ultimately spells the difference between personal significance and emptiness, happiness and depression, success and failure. Examining and experiencing who He really is and what He really thinks about you is fundamental to getting unstuck

1 http://religion.blogs.cnn.com/2010/11/12/our-take-your-relationship-style-determines-how-you-feel-toward-god/

from self-defeating thoughts and behaviors, dissatisfaction with yourself, and unfulfilling or harmful relationships.

It starts by accepting and embracing God's perfect goodness. As your adopted Dad, God is always good. He's not waiting for you to mess up so He can beat you up. He's not shaking His head in disappointment about you. God is the kind of good that lifts your head with a gentle finger to your chin and counts you worthy to look you full in the eyes. He is the kind of good that overlooks where you have been and what you have done and sees you only as His.

I worked with Charlotte for several months, helping her set appropriate limits on harmful people and self-destructive behavior, administer needed self-care, and view her life through the lens of goodness that occasionally surprised her with glimmers of light and hope. She began to acknowledge her career accomplishments, and her self-talk became more positive. Charlotte started calling the goodness she had experienced "God." Her new God rarely resembled the shaming God she heard about growing up and saw in her parents. And whenever she did perceive God that way, she learned to acknowledge that those messages were from her mother and father, not from God at all.

Charlotte began to make real progress and evidenced a marked improvement in her depression. Around this time, I was planning a long maternity leave and needed to refer her to another counselor. At our last session, she was understandably reluctant to say goodbye. "This is where I first found hope, Michelle. I'm afraid it will go away or that I'll forget how to find it."

I felt compelled to say, “My calling is to be the hands and feet of Jesus to the people I meet. You are not alone, Charlotte. Hope has found you.”

A couple of years later, Charlotte contacted me. She was managing her depression well, had made some supportive friends and had recently begun instructing junior dancers, which she loved. She said that God was more real to her than ever before, and that God was indeed good.

“Remember when you told me about being Jesus’ hands and feet?” she said. “I want to know more about Him.” Her second act was about to begin.

“The Lord is good and his love endures for ever; his faithfulness continues through all generations” (Psalm 100:5 NIV). What if your thinking and acting began to reflect the reality that God is truly and perfectly good? How would that change your life? How would it alter your relationship with Him? How would it affect your view of yourself? God is better than you think. Don’t let the pain of the past stop you from growing into your bright future as the dearly loved child of a good, good God.

Questions for Self Reflection:

- What distorted thoughts about God have you had in the past?
- How did church or organized religion play a part in those distortions?
- Have you ever tried really hard to get someone to love you?
- Have you felt like you had to earn love? How and from whom?
- What was one of your first experiences of feeling God? How did you know it was Him?

Intention Statement:

Today, I will not only believe *that God loves me, I will* act *like it too.*

Extra Study:

2 Chronicles 6:14; Psalms 109:21; Isaiah 46:7-13

three

God Is Love, but Not the Kind You're Used To

God loves us—not because He wants us to be really good people, but because He wants us to be really loved people. Loved people change the world.

I'm a tea drinker and there is a particular way I like my tea. For the best taste, the water used must be piping hot. The tea bag must be able to steep for at least 90 seconds but no longer than three minutes. This allows the water to become infused with the tea leaves, but not become too bitter. Ok, so I'm not really a tea drinker, I'm a tea snob.

Back in the day, tea became popular because the water was just too gross to drink by itself. If the tea was too weak, it was useless because you could still taste the terrible water. Knowing about God's love but not really experiencing it is like drinking weak tea. Your life never really gets infused with God's love, and you still taste sort of gross. You may hold on to the theoretical love that says, "Jesus loves me this I know, because the Bible tells me so," all the while experiencing very little of the real thing in tangible ways.

So what does it matter? Why is God's love important, anyway? Like the infant who suffers from "failure to thrive" without necessary love and care, God's children are failing to thrive because they haven't embraced their Father's love. He reaches down with gobs of it dripping from His fingers, but we are too scared or too proud to claim it for ourselves.

To thrive, an intentional move toward letting God love you all the way through is crucial.

Jordan's Story

Jordan was a successful thirty-four-year-old with a promising career in sales. He was talented, respected and promotable, but riddled with stress and anxiety. It permeated everything he did. He couldn't sleep and had chronic stomach problems. He thought obsessively about work. Constructive feedback from his boss would send him into a self-loathing spiral. He became increasingly isolated, exhausted and distrusting of others. That's when his anxiety turned into depression.

During our sessions together, Jordan challenged some of his unrealistic expectations of himself, and worked on taking care of his anxiety symptoms. We also talked about the God-figures in his life that were hard to please, unpredictable and less than affirming. This was a great start, but something else Jordan did stimulated the process to a new level.

About this time, Jordan met a man roughly his father's age, named Oliver. They played golf together on Saturdays.

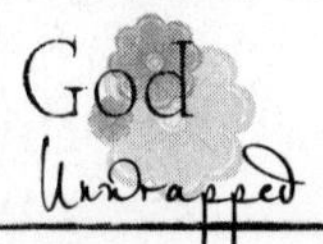

Oliver was a successful businessman from Jordan's church. Jordan respected him, and without even knowing it, Oliver became a new God-figure to Jordan. They golfed for a couple of months, and within the context of this relationship, Jordan began to feel accepted and valued for who he was, not just what he could produce. The past fears of being a disappointment unraveled in the safety of this new relationship. Jordan started to share some of his work stresses with Oliver. Oliver would say things like, "Oh yeah, I've felt that way before too," and "There was this one time I screwed up so bad...," and "I think they're lucky to have you."

Over time, Jordan made a conscious decision to entertain the idea that what Oliver said just might be true. He let Oliver's affirmations infuse his thinking and they changed the way he thought about himself. Jordan's ideas of performance-based love were challenged, and the anxiety of not measuring up began to dissipate. Jordan started to let himself be human instead of perfect. The more he steeped himself in this God-kind of love, the freer from anxiety he became, just like the Bible says, "Perfect love drives out fear..."(1 John 4:18 NIV).

Next are some characteristics to help you determine if you have really let God love you all the way through.

You know you're not infused with God's love if you feel...

Competition and comparisons: When you haven't experienced a secure love, you are *in*secure. You may compare yourself with other people and judge them to be better or worse than you. Judging others always puts you in a catch-22 situation because you end up feeling superior on one hand or inferior on the other—a real lose-lose situation. A silent

competition ensues that eventually brings jealousy, division and isolation from others.

Inside you say, "I don't know who I am until I know how I measure up to other people. I'm afraid that I am not good enough to be truly loved."

Hiding out in isolation: If you haven't been infused with God's love, you feel a deep sense of shame. You feel as though you can't be accepted just the way you are, so you end up disconnecting with others. I moved a lot as a child and with each move, I became more and more shy. Because I was afraid that the kids at the new school wouldn't like me, I isolated myself from them. I avoided the risk of being rejected by limiting connection.

Inside you say, "I'm afraid that you will see who I really am, and then reject me. I can't bear that so I will never show you who I really am."

Deprivation Affect: You worry about God meeting your needs. You don't believe that God is good enough to help you face the challenges in your life. You feel as if you have been deprived of the things that would make you "enough." This belief system keeps you from being everything that God meant you to be.

Inside you say, "I'm afraid of not being good enough to be loved or successful enough to be respected. Since I don't have what it takes, I'll think of excuses not to try."

Punitive Indictment: You worry that your mistakes or evil sin nature will earn you God's silence or punishment, and you see difficult circumstances as God's displeasure with you. You feel like your desires are bad, gluttonous, selfish and prideful, and ought to be squelched, stomped and seared.

Inside you say, "Bad things happen to me because I just can't get it right. I deserve God's wrath."

Immaturity reigns: You haven't applied the discipline of God's love to your life and so you feel entitled and ultimately disappointed. You don't associate the natural consequences of life to the choices you make. You see yourself as a victim of circumstance placed precariously at the center of the universe, and God as a cosmic kill-joy.

Inside you say, "Bad things happen to me because other people just don't appreciate who I really am. Doesn't God hear me?"

You know you're infused with God's love if you feel:

Collaboration and Cooperation: When you are infused with love, you are able to invite others into your life without intimidation or comparison. You want to collaborate instead of compete. A collaborative marriage, for example, is one where both individuals operate not out of fear of losing themselves, but out of love to gain the other.

Inside you say, "Because I am accepted and loved just as I am, I can accept and love you just as you are. We are not competitors, we are friends."

Togetherness: When you are infused with love, you are motivated to connect with other people. You risk being authentic with others because you know that what you have is worth sharing. You reach out to others, seek to build relationships, and stay connected to people even through disappointment and pain.

Inside you say, "I am free to be who I really am, even when I make mistakes. My mistakes don't have to keep me from connecting with others."

Abundance: When you are love-infused, you have a sense of sufficiency. You know that you have enough time, enough resources, enough energy and enough….life for doing life. Jesus said, "I have come that they may have life, and that they may have it more abundantly" (John 10:10 NKJV). You recognize your own needs and make choices to provide for them.

Inside you say, "I have everything I need to fulfill my purpose. I have enough for what I need, what I want and enough to give away."

Discipline is Training: You see God's hand extended with provision, not punishment. You see yourself as a responsible partner in the plan of God's abundance—a runner in the race, with God as your coach. You see discipline as the Bible describes it, "God's discipline is always good for us, so that we might share in his holiness. No discipline is enjoyable while it is happening—it's painful! But afterward there will be a peaceful harvest of right living for those who are trained in this way" (Hebrews 12:10-11 NLT). You see God's discipline as a natural outflow of His love for you so you can accomplish your deepest desires.

Inside you say, "These difficulties are prepping me for my next great adventure with Christ."

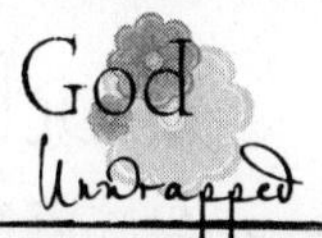

Spiritual Maturity: When you are infused with God's love, you have allowed the wisdom, discipline and words of God to transform you completely. What trapped you, troubled you and tripped you up in the past no longer has the power to do so because you know yourself to be an overcomer. Because you have taken God's love in for yourself, you are able to give it freely and unconditionally to others.

Inside you say, "God has provided for me in the past, and He will continue to do so. I no longer live for myself, but I live for God and His service."

Questions for Self Reflection:

- In your life, who has been an example of God's unconditional love?
- When do you feel competitive with others? Collaborative?
- When do you feel isolated? A sense of togetherness?
- When do you feel like you're living in deprivation? Abundance?
- When do you feel punished by God or self? When do you feel trained or disciplined?
- What good and not-so-good things did the god-figures in your life teach you about love? What have you had to un-learn?
- In what areas of your life do you need love most? (i.e. relational hurts, professional short-comings, past hurts)

Intention Statement:

Today I will choose to take hold of God's love instead of 'failing to thrive'. Today, I will not only believe *that God loves me, I will* act *like it too.*

Extra Study:

1 John 4:13-21; Deuteronomy 7:9; Psalm 51:1

four

The Kindergarten Teacher

"Come back to the LORD your God, because he is kind and shows mercy."

Joel 2:13 NCV

Do you remember your kindergarten teacher? Mine was plump and soft and warm. I remember her salt-and-pepper hair and her name: Mrs. Smith. She did the things that kindergarten teachers are supposed to do: teach letters and numbers, help you tie your shoes, and make a safe place to learn and play and come to every day. Mrs. Smith did those things. One day, she helped my mom look for me after school when I secretly decided to ride the bus to a friend's house instead of walking home. I got in trouble later when they found me, and I remember not regretting my decision at all except that I made Mrs. Smith worried. I felt bad about that because I liked her.

Our English word "kind" is related to the German word "kinder," meaning "child." Think of "kindergarten," literally "a garden of children." Children need a measure of kindness,

because they are fragile and vulnerable and need the right kind of environment to grow healthy and strong. This may be what all children need, but it is not always what they get, and it's the latter that needs some attention.

Michael's Story

Cordial and brimming with business savvy, Michael came to me not long ago for executive coaching. Sixty-five years old and never married, he had enjoyed a long, respected, and productive career in the company he helped build. Michael's partners had referred him to me to help him work out an exit strategy for his upcoming retirement. During our get-acquainted session, Michael kept talking about his company and accomplishments. When I asked what he thought about retirement, he gazed off into space for a few seconds. "Retirement is not my idea," he said at last. "My partners want me to retire."

It took a few weeks before Michael felt safe enough to talk about his problem with retirement. "I'm just not ready, Michelle. I have so much more to do. The company will falter if I'm not there."

"But you told me that you were comfortable with the man you hired to take your place," I countered. "You said he was the right person for the job."

"Yes, he's good. But there are so many loose ends to tie up, so many things that only *I* know about."

"This isn't making sense to me, Michael," I said. "You've been wrapping up unfinished business at the office for some time now. You say you trust your partners and like the new guy coming in. You've been telling me about your vacation plans. And now you're not ready? What's this about?"

Michael drew a long breath and released it slowly. "Do you know why I pour so many hours into my work, Michelle?"

"Tell me," I said.

"Because I have nobody who needs me to do other things besides work. And do you know why I don't have people who need me? Because I can't keep them. Once I get to know someone I start feeling uncomfortable, so I do something terrible to break off the relationship. That's what this is all about."

Now we were getting somewhere.

"Something terrible?" I probed.

"Yeah, like I don't return phone calls or I pretend to lose interest or I dive into work so I won't have time."

I proceeded slowly, sensitive to the fact that Michael had just bared his soul. "So you are afraid to retire because you'll be alone, right?" Michael responded with a slight nod. "And you are alone because you're afraid of...what, exactly?"

"I'm afraid I'll be rejected." It was all Michael could say. He dropped his head and tried to keep from crying.

After a few moments of silence I asked, "Michael, what do you know about rejection?"

He talked briefly about a mother who provided for him in many ways but lacked the kindness of affection and

encouragement. He recalled his mother flinching at his overtures for closeness. During adolescence Michael suffered from severe acne, causing him to isolate from peers and suppress his interest in girls. Ashamed of how he looked, one day he reached out to his mother for support. "Mom, do you think I look okay?"

She replied, "It doesn't really matter what I say, does it?"

Like a rock to glass, young Michael's budding self-concept was shattered by his mother's indifference. He walled up his heart and poured his energies into what he knew he could do well. He achieved good grades and got through college on sports scholarships. As an adult, his face cleared up and he dated many women, but all his relationships were short-lived by his choice. In the eyes of others, Michael was a dynamic, hard-charging, handsome man. But on the inside, he was an emotional teenager terrified of being rejected, especially by women.

Sadly, Michael's reaction to the lack of kindness from his mother is all too common. We tend to do to ourselves what has been done to us. From an early age, we learned how to respond to others, based on how they responded to us. We mirrored others as a means of making sense of our world and our own place within it. Expressions, gestures and visual cues are imprinted in the mind in the same way that emotional messages and meaning are imprinted on the soul. We learn our value in the context of familial relationships. These relationships have the power to impart and imprint worth and love, or worthlessness and insecurity.

If you grew up experiencing parental neglect, criticism, or shame—whether blatant or subtle—you probably began treating yourself the same way at an early age. Even as an adult you may beat yourself up when you make mistakes or cave in to the wishes of others instead of standing up for yourself. For instance, if you experienced feeling unwanted in the past, you may perpetuate the cycle today by pursuing people who don't want you. Unconsciously you feel that if you can finally get them to like/love you, then you'll finally have arrived at being lovable.

Many Christians try to legitimize their self-deprecating behavior as godly and humble. Why? Because they tend to view God as a disapproving parent who is always disappointed in them. I hear people say things like, "God really hammered me" or "God came after me with a two-by-four," or "God wants me to be single and that's why He hasn't sent me the one." Who wants to warm up to a God who uses hammers, two-by-fours and natural selection to correct His children?

God is not like Michael's mother or anyone in your life who marginalizes you for how you look, what you do, or some trumped-up pecking order. God is not a disapproving or un-involved parent. The apostle Paul writes, "When God our Savior revealed his kindness and love, he saved us, not because of the righteous things we had done, but because of his mercy. He washed away our sins, giving us a new birth and new life through the Holy Spirit" (Titus 3:4-5 NLT). God says, "When Israel was a child, I loved him, and I called my son out of Egypt" (Hosea 11:1 NLT) and, "I myself taught

Israel[2] how to walk, leading him along by the hand. But he doesn't know or even care that it was I who took care of him. I led Israel along with my ropes of kindness and love. I lifted the yoke from his neck, and I myself stooped to feed him" (Hosea 11:3-4 NLT).

Think about Jesus welcoming the children who toddled up to Him. When His disciples wanted to shoo the little pests away, Jesus simply said, "The kingdom of heaven belong to such as these" (Matthew 19:14 NIV).

God reaches across heaven to His children and offers kindness and compassion at precisely the time we feel our most awkward, ugly, sinful, or unwanted. In fact, it's when we are farthest away from Him that we need His kindness the most. The Bible tells us that it is God's kindness—not His anger or disappointment or criticism—that leads us to change for the better (see Romans 2:4).

However, borrowing the old saying, God can lead you to the water of kindness that transforms, but He can't make you drink it. I mean, forcing His kindness on you kind of defeats His purpose, doesn't it? You have to receive His kindness personally and let it transform how you think about yourself, talk to yourself, and treat yourself. As you allow yourself to absorb kindness, you'll be able to lighten up on yourself and everybody else.

A female client came to me a few years ago with self-image issues. She didn't like her looks in general and hated her thighs in particular. She never felt good enough growing up, and so

2 Hebrew *Ephraim,* referring to the northern kingdom of Israel; also in 11:8, 9, 12.

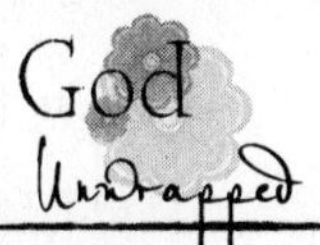

she picked the worst behaving parts of her body to hate. She would scowl at them in the mirror, call them terrible names, and thoroughly chastise them for not fitting into jeans easier. After assuring her that God didn't have a problem with the way she looked, but rather was *partial* to it, I gave her an assignment. I told her to go buy some expensive skin cream and massage it into her thighs every day, saying to them, "I'm so thankful for you, thighs. I'm sorry for complaining about you and saying you aren't good enough for me. After all, you dimply, jiggly things get me around every day, and I love ya'!"

My client laughed and said it was a crazy idea. But that's the fun part of my job, seeing if my clients will do the crazy things I suggest. Of course, this is not the way most people respond to their weaknesses and faults. But God in His infinite kindness specializes in meeting us right where we hurt the most, and transforming weakness and ugliness into strength and beauty. He looks at those thighs and says, "They are good! Now, get them moving and make a difference in My world!"

I encouraged Michael, my business coaching client, to start replacing his mother's shaming messages with the truth he needed as a boy: "Son, you are a handsome, strapping young man just beginning to develop. These awkward changes in your body will only last a short time. You are a great guy inside and out, and any girl with half a brain would feel lucky to go out with you. Even though you can't see what a treasure you are, I can see it, blast it, and don't you ever forget it!"

That's the kind heart of God in action. We all need God to show up for us like a compassionate mom. We need God to be nurturing and wise and soft and available. We need God to be aware of our embarrassing attributes and shortcomings and be completely devoted to us just the same. And sometimes we need God to get all mama-bear, telling us like it is. In our most vulnerable state, when we ask Him, "Am I okay?" God replies, "You're not just okay; you're Mine!"

As Michael began exchanging shame and hurt for true kindness, he began to open up to others. He eventually retired from the company and actually started dating again. He pushed through the discomfort of his nagging self-doubt to begin living like the adult he knew himself to be, instead of the wounded little boy from a long time ago. And my wonderful thigh client? Her thighs are the last thing on her mind. She is too busy launching her new art studio.

Show some kindness to the parts of yourself that give you the most disappointment. When you do, you will be acting in harmony with the kindness of your heavenly Father.

Questions for Self Reflection:

- What parts of yourself disappoint you?
- How do you still reenact patterns from the past?
- What past mistakes do you regret to the point of unforgiveness?
- What unkind actions and messages from god-figures bring shame and doubt still today?
- Write down God's kind answer to that unkindness.

Intention Statement:

God is always kind toward me, and is always looking at me with compassion.

Extra Study:

Ephesians 2:7; Colossians 3:12; Galatians 5:22; Hosea 11:1-11

God
Unwrapped

five

Does God Get Mad?

"Love is not irritable...."

1 Corinthians 13:5 NLT

Richard Dawkins, atheist and author of *The God Delusion*, gives the description of God as "the most unpleasant character in all fiction ... a misogynist, homophobic, racist, infanticidal, genocidal, filicidal, pestilential, megalomaniacal, sadomasochistic, capriciously malevolent bully."[3] Though as Christians we would say otherwise, sometimes we have so misinterpreted God's "wrathful" side that we act like we agree with Mr. Dawkins.

In high school, I was assigned to write a report on a Puritan figure and I chose Jonathan Edwards, creator of the well known sermon, "Sinners in the Hands of an Angry God." He attracted waves of frightened loyalists as he depicted wicked men and women dangling above an open pit of fire

3 Dawkins, Richard. *The God Delusion*. Great Britain: Bantam Press, 2006.

suspended by the hand of an angry God. I think that is where we came up with the slogan, "Turn or Burn." I remember being relieved that my pastor didn't preach like him. In fact, my pastor at the time was so kind and grandfatherly, that upon interviewing him for my report, I assumed he would denounce Edwards' obsession with brimstone. I was surprised and confused when he was remarkably positive toward Edwards. My confusion about God's anger followed me into adulthood as I wrestled with my own anger issues. I'm not a red head for nothing.

God's anger is not like the anger we have witnessed or experienced from our own god-figures. At the risk of sounding trite, God's anger is always for our good. We hear something like this and it brings us back to the spanking of childhood when the parent said something like, "I'm doing this for your own good," and we couldn't quite believe it. But let me explain it further.

God hurts.

Anger is a secondary emotion. Hurt is always at the core of anger. When a person is hurt, he can turn outwardly in anger, or inwardly in depression. God's primary emotion toward humanity when something has gone wrong is *hurt*. God hurts *for* us and *with* us, and sometimes *because* of us. But God is able to contain that hurt and respond to it appropriately.

God, unlike us, is completely self-controlled. A good example of this self control is the account of Jesus' trial and death. He was tried under false pretenses, sentenced to die in place of a murderer, beaten, spit upon, sneered at, mocked and tortured with crucifixion. Through all this excruciating and humiliating treatment, He did not react in anger but said, "Father, forgive them, for they do not know what they do" (Luke 23:34 NKJV).

God doesn't have dependency issues.

Sometimes we get mad at other people because we depend on them too much. Children must depend on their parents for survival. This is healthy and good. But as we mature, we must transfer those dependencies to God and not look to others to fill the needs our parents never could. If we depend on other people to fill those needs in ways only God can, then we are consistently disappointed and become hurt and angry.

Since God doesn't *need* us for anything, He does not get embarrassed by us, and He never gets disappointed in us. God does not get angry with His children because they are messing up His plans, His life, or His stuff. He gets angry when they are messing up *their* lives. Godly anger is born out of love—love for us.

He is not mad or hurt because our rebellion or rejection affects Him. He is angry because our rebellion and rejection affects *us*. In fact, God is rightly ticked off when we destroy ourselves and others at the altars of false gods and empty promises.

God *Is* Mad at Injustice

When I was younger, my family spent some time in the livestock business. We raised and sold sheep. We lived in the country and I learned my fair share about trailer-livin', leased land, castration, sheep dogs, and ranch chores.

On one particular spring morning, I experienced something I'll never forget. I arrived at the lambing stalls and began my chores. It was a cold Colorado morning and I remember wondering how many lambs made it through the night. I mixed formula with warm water and set to feeding the bum lambs. We had a lot of bum lambs that year. The ewes were old and sickly and seemed down-right cantankerous. Some lambs were born dead, others would die soon after. Some ewes were too weak and died during birth. Some didn't have the milk supply to feed their lambs. It was a bad year.

Some ewes, the bitter ones, tried killing their lambs the moment they arrived, maybe instinctually knowing they didn't have what it took to feed them, I don't know. A lamb, still steaming and wet from birth, would teeter onto its legs just long enough for the ewe to butt it into the side of the wooden stall. Then, as the confused lamb tried to get up again, its mother would stomp it with her hooves until it stopped moving. Some ewes were less overtly aggressive and would move away from their lambs just as they started to suckle, slowly starving them of the milk they needed.

Many lambs died that spring—too many to keep up with actually. I remember the pile of the dead growing each day—one limp body on top of another.

That cold morning, while warming the bottles, I heard some shouting and banging at the other end of the stalls. Two of the ranch hands were standing by, watching a scene unfold in front of them, stunned. My dad was having it out with one of the ewes. I had watched him jar a ewe or two before. I never liked it—it seemed so terrible. But, after "getting their attention," he would take the lamb, hold the ewe down, and let the lamb suck. This worked with a few of the crotchety ewes. It was like they had to get "used to" the idea of being a mother again.

But this ewe had already killed one of her lambs, and was about to do the same to its twin. On that cold morning, I think my dad had enough of the death, enough of the disappointment, and enough of the sickness. Grunting, kicking, bleating, bashing, yelling—I thought the whole pen would crash down. That one ewe was catching hell for all the infanticidal mothers that year.

It was like a scene from a movie that I wanted to hide my eyes from. I didn't know if he would stop. I didn't know if he would win. I wondered, "Is this the way it's done?"

In a moment, he decisively grabbed up the little lamb, still in the stall, and gave him to one of the men standing by. Finally, silence fell except for the mother's heavy breathing. He walked single-mindedly to the pile of dead lambs, and dug his way through until he selected a body. He looked it over, and knelt down. Horrified, I watched him take out his pocket knife and slit the limp body from butt to jaw. He skinned that little dead thing, right there in front of us. All three of us looked on wondering if he had lost his mind.

He tossed the scraps of remains aside and held the scrawny hide up to size it with his eyes. My dad, like a man holding in a hurricane, took the living lamb from the hired hand and fitted the hide snug on top of him. He paced a few stalls over, and set the frightened lamb in a new pen. The ewe in this pen was a young mother whose lamb had died due to the cold or illness, something not due to her own brutality. She sniffed the lamb, turned away and stamped her foot in defiance. She didn't want somebody else's leftovers.

My dad would not be outdone—not this day. He jumped in the crowded, manure-smeared stall, and held that lamb firmly in front of the young ewe's snout. He petted the ewe, he talked kindly to her, and began to convince her that this was really her little lamb. And in fact, the living lamb was wearing her dead lamb's skin—how my father found it in the pile I don't know. Desperation can give a keen sense of awareness.

He petted the ewe some more. Finally, the young mother licked it. My dad's shoulders gave way in a sigh. "Here's your lamb, come on, here he is." He took the lamb to the underside of the ewe, and for the first time in days, the lamb began to suckle without threat.

My dad, with hair in his eyes, and red on his face, was suddenly aware that he had an audience. He stood up and announced to the gaping observers, "That lamb needed a mother." He strode off. The pain in my father's face made it clear that this day would never be discussed.

Just Love

There is a brutality to the love of God—there is a determination on the side of justice and righteousness, a fortitude that refuses to let die what was meant for living. That is God's heart for us. God will not give up. He, with fury, unleashed the wrath of the murderous ages beginning with the murder of Abel, to the murder of His tender Lamb, and with one stroke, His wrath was laid on His own Son. Jesus took on this wrath willingly, because He could do nothing *but* love us.

It's as if He saved us from the mother who couldn't love us, and fitted us with Christ's sacrifice so that we could live. Christ announced, "This people need a Father," and then He lay down His life for our sake.

Whether we identify with the old ewe who can't take it anymore, or the lamb that no one wants, God shows up in His fierceness to provide a way back to Himself. His fierceness is *for* us, not *against* us.[4]

Paul writes to the Romans, "So through Christ we will surely be saved from God's anger, because we have been made right with God by the blood of Christ's death. While we were God's enemies, he made us his friends through the death of his Son. Surely, now that we are his friends, he will save us through his Son's life. And not only that, but now we are also very happy in God through our Lord Jesus Christ. Through him we are now God's friends again" (Romans 5:9-11 NCV).

We do not have to fear that God's anger burns against us when we sin. He has sworn to never be angry with us again. (Isaiah 54:9-10 NIV).

---

4 Peterson, Eugene H. *The Message : The Bible in Contemporary Language.* Colorado Springs, Colo. : NavPress, 2002. S. 1 Thessalonians 5:9-10 "God didn't set us up for an angry rejection but for salvation by our Master, Jesus Christ. He died for us, a death that triggered life."

Questions for Self Reflection:

- How have you visualized God's anger in the past?
- Who in your past has dealt with you out of anger?
- What triggers your anger? What do you do with it? Stuff it, yell it, or project it onto others?
- Can you envision using that energy for something positive?
- What would it be like to see everything in the light of God's love, instead of God's wrath? How would your life be different?

Intention Statement:

God isn't mad at me because I am human. Today, I will be reminded of God's smile toward me.

Extra Study:

Psalm 86:15; Hosea 11:9; James 1:20

six

Three-Miles-Per-Hour

"Love is patient..."

1 Corinthians 13:4 NIV

My husband, Brian, makes fun of me because I can watch the most boring stuff on TV and be completely entertained. One day, I found the channel that broadcasts live from the Senate chamber in Washington, D.C. I was completely mesmerized for 30 minutes watching these people in suits, from a bird's eye view, walk in and out of the cherry-wood paneled room. Like Mowgli looking directly into Kaa's eyes, I was hooked. Oh, and they were in recess. Brian, with disdain for the "trash" I watch, often comes in and says, "There *must* be something better on," and then will channel surf for an hour. I think my way is better.

One day, on an alluringly boring channel, I saw a panel of world religious leaders, discussing common challenges that people have. Watching boring religious stuff is my all-time fave—and you're going to be thankful it is because of the next juicy detail I'm about to tell you.

A question was raised, "How can an individual not be so hard on himself when he makes a mistake?" The Dali Lama was there, Rob Bell, author of *Velvet Elvis* was there—and some other people I didn't recognize—and they all took their turns answering. Arch Bishop Tutu was there too, and he described God as a parent teaching His child to walk. Each time the child fell, God would dust the child off and say with a smile, "It's ok, try again." Then the Arch Bishop said, "This God does not say, 'Good riddance to bad rubbish!' This God is a three-mile-per-hour God. He walks at our pace."

This made me think of the time I put my eldest daughter in swimming lessons when she was four, mainly because I mistakenly believed, "four year olds should know how to swim." As the lessons grew in difficulty and discomfort for my daughter, she became more resistant. She began to regress instead of progress, and began dreading swimming lesson day. She completed the scheduled lessons that summer, having never submerged her head in the water. As much as I wanted to force her to learn to swim, my sanity returned and by family decision, she skipped the next season's lessons.

Over the next two years, she voluntarily experimented with goggles, floaties, and plugging her nose in the bath tub. Then, two years after swimming lessons, she, on her own accord, began to swim.

For her, swimming had been something scary and difficult. Forcing her to swim before she was ready would have hurt both of us, and provoked some real resentment and shame in her as well. Healthy growth never comes out of being coerced, shamed, or forced. Had my daughter learned

to swim under those negative circumstances, she would have done so at the cost of her budding sense of self.

We are the ones in a hurry, not God.

We are impatient with ourselves, and we think we should be doing better in life. We may even think that God is frustrated with our slow progress, and is expecting more from us. So, we feel bad about ourselves. We act out in subtle ways, like sulking and whining, and resenting other people who are "further along."

But God doesn't force us to do things that we are not ready to do. Maybe other people around us are impatient with us, or maybe the voices of our past say we "should hurry up already," but that is not God's voice.

God does expect growth—because growth is a sign of life. If you're not dead, God expects you to grow. But His ways of growth may not be what you think.

Ways of Growth

Firstly, God organizes some *internal processes* in the human psyche for forward movement and maturity. We see this in the child who wants to learn to potty train, the teen who wants to drive, the thirty-something mom who takes art classes, or the middle-aged man who wants to learn to fly. God has designed us to grow, expand, and flourish. This drive is a part of who we are.

Secondly, God organizes some *external stimuli* for growth. In the case of my daughter, in addition to her own desire to

learn new things, she saw the kids around her having a lot of fun in the water. She saw the possibilities that learning the new skill would provide and decided to give it a try. She also experienced the pain of not growing, as she watched her younger sister gaining on her in water proficiency.

God allows both the painful consequences of the natural world and the internal pang for more, to get us ready for growth. He honors us uniquely and understands, much more than we do, that each of us is ready for growth in our own time. He nurtures us, helping us to feel safe and grounded, and He challenges us to take the next step.

Why Growing is Daunting

When I was six, I wanted to jump from the high dive. I eyed that looming board from below every week until I asked my swim instructor for permission to try it. She obliged, encouraging my sense of adventure, and told me she'd wait for me at the bottom. I could barely tread water, let alone swim, but I wanted to do the things I saw the big people do. For three weeks straight, I climbed the ladder with wobbly legs and stood at the top of the board. There, with the world before me, the florescent lights above, *and a watery tomb below*, I stood. I waited. I counted to three … 15 times. I spotted my instructor waiting for me to jump. And then I climbed back down the ladder. Three lessons straight, this scenario occurred and three times my swim instructor smiled and said I could try again when I was ready. Then one day I jumped. I have an idea now what finally made me do it. I waited until I knew it was a safe place to fail, before I decided to succeed. My teacher's resolute patience made it safe.

God gives us the desire to grow and become like Christ, and He waits until our desire matches His. It is His patience in the face of our fear that finally gives us the courage to take the plunge.

The trick to being ready is to get in touch with the desire to become who we really are—to finally be free of the shame and fear that has kept us bound. By listening to ourselves and validating the desire inside, we start to trust ourselves and trust God. We start to believe that learning to walk is less about the falling and more about the *experience* with the Father: Him smiling, us trying, Him encouraging, us losing balance, and Him dusting us off and encouraging us to try again. The relationship is primary, the learning to walk is secondary. That's the way the Three-Mile-Per-Hour God designed it.

Questions for Self Reflection:

- In what areas of your life would you like to receive God's patience for yourself?
- Have you given yourself permission to fail before?
- Write down the desires you have that are unfulfilled because of fear of failure.
- How are you resisting the growth and fulfillment God wants for you?
- In what areas of your life are you moving faster than God? How do you know?

Intention Statement:

Today I will choose to be less results-oriented, and more process-oriented. I will allow myself the patience to be on the journey, learning as I go. Today I will be patient with myself.

Extra Study:

1 Corinthians 13:4, 11-13; Romans 2:4

seven

Truth or Fiction

[Love]...rejoices whenever the truth wins out.

1 Corinthians 13:6 NLT

My grandmother, Mildred, lived with us a few years when I was in high school. Thinking about her makes me smile. She kept her money in her bra. So, when we stood at the counter in a store, she took her sweet time to reach down the neck of her dress fishing for dollar bills and coins to pay. The look on the clerk's face was always worth the wait. She loved to wear hats to church, get her hair done at the salon, and smear Ponds cream an inch think on her face at bedtime. In the morning before an outing, she would puff powder all over her face, neck and glasses. The powder would cling to the oily prints left on the lenses from her Ponds-y fingers the night before. Sometimes, I would sneak into her room just to clean her glasses so she could see her crosswords better. Despite these endearing quirks, every person in our family would point to Grandma Middy as being a key reason why they know about Jesus today. She was the one who got to know Him first.

Those smudgy glasses come to mind when I think about our own ability to see truth. Our view of ourselves is a little greasy, and our view of God is dim. This has to do with our past, our fears, our human nature, and the darkness of the father of lies. Satan is pleased as punch when we are blinded to the truth. In fact, he works tirelessly puffing his powder to keep us from seeing clearly.

Jessica's Story

Take Jessica for instance. Jessica had one young child with a second on the way. She worked as a pastoral counselor for women in her church. She fought depression most of her life, and when she came to see me, she admitted that she had "managed" her depression with exercise and Bible study. I wondered if she was the "just pray more" type.

When she became pregnant with her second child, she was overwhelmed. Depression began to settle in like an unwanted guest with no plans for leaving. She fought the very thought of depression, saying to herself, "I am not supposed to be depressed, I am supposed to be happy. I should be more thankful!" She had tried anti-depressants before with positive results, but not long after, she convinced herself that she should be able to manage her depression on her own, and threw the pills away. A well meaning but delusional friend had even advised her that dependency on drugs and counseling was actually a sign that she wasn't trusting God enough. Excuse me while I vomit in my mouth.

Her denial of the depression's severity and longevity kept her in a state of disappointment with God and with herself.

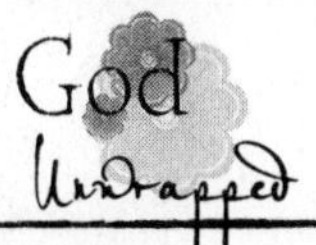

She questioned the quality of her faith and the promises of God. She knew that it was ok for Christians to struggle, but she never let it be ok for *her* to struggle—after all, she counseled women who struggled, so she was supposed to have it all together. No matter how hard she tried to deny it, the truth was that she was depressed.

Once she talked through her unrealistic expectations of herself, she discovered that she had many unmet needs. She needed to be accepted and valued just as she was, not for what she produced. She needed to be loved, even when she didn't measure up to her expectations. She realized that she had spent her life shaming herself for having these needs, and she had worked hard to deny them.

She relayed information about her mother who lived with untreated depression. Her father, a minister, labored tediously at hiding her mother's depression, making it seem to the outside world that the family was perfect. Jessica had learned that depression was unacceptable and a shameful sign of spiritual weakness—something that good Christians just shouldn't have.

Sometimes, I get the great pleasure of watching a client "get it." I know this "get it" feeling myself. It's God wiping the lenses clean. I watched Jessica get it. She said, "I'm figuring out that this depression doesn't mean that I'm a fraud or a bad Christian. It just means that I need to take care of myself. And that's actually ok." The tear that sparked her eye and the smile that crept onto her lips was God himself rejoicing in the truth. She accepted the reality that she had legitimate needs, and that God would help her do something about them.

The magic of accepting the truth.

With her doctor's guidance, she started anti-depressants. Within a few weeks, her baby was born. She commented later that she was able to be fully present and attentive to her new infant because she had accepted the help she needed. She accepted grace for herself, and was able to serve her baby in the way she had always wanted. She also allowed other people to see her true self—the self that didn't have it all together all the time. Their love and acceptance validated her.

When we join with God to bring our true selves up to where we and others can see it, He rejoices with the truth and makes His strength perfect in our weakness (2 Corinthians 12:9 NKJV). He will not do it the other way around. He won't give us strength to push our true selves further down.

We have a real and present enemy who works against the truth. Jesus spoke about Satan as a murderer and a hater of truth (John 8:42-48 NLT). His lies are so akin to our own human makeup and spoon-feed our human arrogance so agreeably, that we don't even recognize them—until the pain of believing them becomes too unbearable.

In Jessica's case, she was caught up in the pride of doing life on her own and believing somehow she could attain perfection. The lie fed the depression and kept her isolated and filled with self-blame. The devil's schemes are designed to keep us bound, trapped, and hopelessly self-reliant. The Bible teaches, "For our struggle is not against flesh and blood… but against the powers of this dark world" (Ephesians 6:11-13 NIV). This verse reminds us that our battle is not against ourselves or with other people, but really against the darkness of this world. That darkness encroaches upon us in subtle ways.

My husband knows about encroachment. Ask him about our shared bathroom counter. I'm a product girl. I like my products. And my products like their space. Lotions, glosses, earrings, nifty disposable tooth brushes and bobby pins inch across the counter top, silently, gaining ground undetectably, until they swallow his sink up in surrender.

This is how the darkness of Satan works too; encroaching on the clean space of our minds until it's cluttered with doubt and fear. The Bible instructs us to not fight against ourselves when this happens, but to realize that our spiritual enemy is on the move and to "stand firm." I'm not even going to repeat what my husband says as he "stands firm" on his side of the bathroom. But use your imagination, and then talk back to the devil in the same way. It's your space, after all.

"So Jesus said to the Jews who believed in him, 'If you continue to obey my teaching, you are truly my followers. Then you will know the truth, and the truth will make you free'" (Ephesians 11:13 NIV).

Questions for Self Reflection:

- What are some truths about yourself that have been difficult to accept?
- If you accepted those truths, how would it change your life?
- How will you find help for your weaknesses?
- Who will you confide in about your secret struggles?
- How has the darkness of this world encroached on your territory?

Intention Statement:

Today, I will accept the truth of who I am—the strong, the weak, and the in-between—and I will grow in the light of that truth, accepting help whenever I need it.

Extra Study:

John 8:31-32; Hebrews 4:12-13;
Proverbs 23:23; Psalm 119:30, 43

eight

Just Because God's in Control, Doesn't Mean He's Controlling

"Keep company with me and you'll learn to live freely and lightly."

Matthew 11:28-30 MSG

I have a friend who spoke honestly about God one day. She said, "Christians always talk about how 'God is in control'. Why would I want someone else in control of my life? It's my life, I want to be in control." I understood what she meant. Just because God is a good driver, doesn't automatically make us want to let Him drive.

Margaret Alter describes it this way, "Psychological evil is the deeply hidden longing in each human to be in absolute control. It presents itself to us at a conscious level quite sensibly as wanting to be safe. But the primitive terror and rage of a small child fuels it. Theologically, it is our battle against our finitude, our longing to be 'like God, knowing good and evil,' as the story of Adam and Eve's temptation in Eden illustrates. While it remains unconscious, we are likely to engage in a variety of controlling behaviors."[5]

Hmm, a "variety of controlling behaviors." Does she mean when I go through my daughters' closets and secretly remove clothes I don't like? Or when my husband is cooking dinner and I come in and take over because I know a better way? Or does she mean how I offer unsolicited advice? I bet what she is really talking about is that one mom at the soccer games who tells the coach what to do.... Oh wait, that's me too. Ok—that's enough self-disclosure, here are some controlling behaviors that I've *never* done myself, but I've *heard* about.

- coercing others into doing our wishes
- throwing adult-sized temper tantrums
- threatening abandonment
- giving the silent treatment
- repeatedly rescuing or saving someone
- restricting another's freedom
- withholding affection or forgiveness
- manipulating with guilt, anger or withdrawal

Controlling people are fearful people. They are afraid that if they let go of control then something bad will happen. They

5 Alter, Margaret, G. *Resurrection Psychology: An Understanding of Human Personality Based on the Life and Teachings of Jesus.* Chicago: Loyala University Press, 1994, P. 151.

are afraid that their marriage, their kids, and they themselves won't be good enough. Being raised by a controlling god-figure can be a very painful experience, leaving you with the feeling that you aren't good, capable, or smart enough to do life yourself. You may end up feeling demeaned and powerless.

Here is what Jesus had to say about it.

In Jesus' day, rabbis interpreted the ancient scripture in attempts to make it functional. These scriptures were to enlighten the people as to their responsibility—their end of the deal. Jesus came against the religious rulers of the day because they had interpreted scripture in a way that burdened the people with unnecessary restrictions and requirements. The rabbis and Pharisees were god-figures to the people, and Jesus didn't like how they represented Him. He was different than the people were used to.

Jesus addressed the weary and burdened people saying, "Take my yoke upon you and learn from me, for I am gentle and lowly in heart, and you will find rest for your souls," (Matthew 11:29 NKJV). The "yoke" is what my friend was talking about. The thought of being yoked like an ox to its master didn't sound good to her, no matter how nice the master was.

But the yoke Jesus was talking about was different. A "yoke" was a garment that rabbis wore around their neck that described *their* interpretation of the scripture. These laws were taught, written down and obeyed with strict adherence. In our lives, we all wear a yoke. We all have interpreted the rules of life in a particular way, and we try to live up to those rules. We believe that living according to that yoke will make us good enough people.

So when Jesus instructs us to wear *His* yoke, He is saying that He will not burden us with unnecessary restrictions or control us with manipulative guilt like the others do. This may have been done to us by controlling people in the past, and we may be doing it to ourselves today, but this isn't true of Jesus.

Remember Abraham? God promised Abraham that he would be the father of an entire nation and he'd have as many descendents as the sky had stars. Abraham waited until he had wrinkles on his wrinkles for God to fulfill that promise. Then God made good on that promise in the form of his son, Isaac. Now, remember when Abraham laid Isaac down on the altar and put the knife to his neck? He was laying down his gift, and his right to the promise. He offered up his will to God the same way Jesus did the night before the crucifixion when He said, "Not my will, but Yours." When we lay down our control on the altar, we are saying to God, "I don't have to control everything. Although You gave me the right to control my life, I lay it down because Your way is better." Once you do this, look for the "ram in the bushes." God always has a substitute sacrifice waiting to be revealed once we surrender control, and it's always something better than we imagined.

The 1986 movie, *The Mission*[6] portrays a broken man, Rodrigo Mendoza, played by Robert Deniro, who is trying to win God's favor. He was a mercenary, murderer, and slave

---

6 Bolt, Robert. *The Mission*. DVD. Directed by Roland Joffé. United Kingdom: Goldcrest Films International, 1986.

trader in South America. Once convicted of his deeds, he felt a heavy remorse. A group of Jesuit priests invited him to travel deep into the jungle as they ministered to the native Guarani tribe—the very tribe he was guilty of murdering and enslaving. He agreed, but only with the condition of a penance. He carried his mercenary armor in a bag behind him, tethered to him with rope, to remind himself of his deeds. Up mountainsides, across deep rivers, through thick forests, he dragged the burden behind him. The weight of the armor almost caused his death several times on the treacherous journey. But he had to be in control. He would not let go.

Atop the mountain, as the group approached the tribe, the priests were greeted as friends, but Mendoza was recognized as the enemy. On hands and knees, covered in mud, Mendoza lay at the mercy of the tribe he had persecuted. A young chief ran to him, put a crude knife to his throat and yelled something to his tribesmen. Mendoza readied himself for his fate. But in a moment, the chief changed position, cut the rope, and kicked the burdensome armor off the cliff into the river below. Not only was his burden thrown down, he was accepted as family among the tribe he previously persecuted.

Letting go of control means letting go of the burden, and it feels like an enormous risk. You may ask, "What if I fail? What if I am judged to be less than adequate? What if God isn't really as good as He says he is?" Only by letting God have access to your burden—your control—will you know Jesus as a *savior*, not as a judge. (John 12:47 NKJV).

Questions for Self Reflection:

- How have you experienced the control of another person? When you are around a controlling person, how do you feel?
- Have you denied a dream because it didn't "fit" a controlling person's expectations of you?
- What controlling behaviors do you demonstrate at work, at home, or with friends? How would your life be different if you surrendered control freely to God?
- What burdens have you been carrying that weigh you down? Perhaps it's a regret from the past, an unbreakable habit, a hidden secret, or the dread of something bad happening.
- Who or what have you been yoked to that has produced unrest, anxiety, or lack of autonomy?

Intention Statement:

Today I will think and behave as a free person. I will use Christ's love as the measure of who and what I am.

Extra Study:

Galatians 4:17; John 10:17-18; Galatians 3:15; John 9:39

nine

The Inmate Inside

"...Because you are strong, and the word of God abides in you, and you have overcome the wicked one."

1 John 2:14c NKJV

I heard a story once about a young woman who complained to her father that her life was too hard. In fact, it was miserable, one hardship after another. She was tired of life always being a struggle.

Her father, having been around the block and no stranger to his own trials, took her to their kitchen. He filled three pots with water and placed them all on high heat. The father rummaged through refrigerator and pantry until he had gathered the necessary items. While the impatient daughter waited, he set eggs into the first boiling pot of water, potatoes in the second, and ground coffee beans in the third.

The two sat in the kitchen until a timer sounded. The father turned off the heat, and asked, "Daughter, what do you see?"

"Eggs, potatoes and coffee."

"Look closer," he said, "touch the potatoes." She did and noted they were soft. He then asked her to take an egg and break it.

After pulling off the shell, she said, "The egg is hard."

The father then ladled coffee from the pot and gave it to his daughter to taste. He said, "Each was put under the same fire for the same amount of time. The hard potatoes became soft. The fragile egg became hard. But the coffee is unique. Do you know why?"

The daughter was finally engaged and listening intently.

"The coffee, under fire, changed its whole environment and created something new."

God Uses Choice-Making Moments to Empower Us

One of the most powerful gifts that God could give people is their own ability to choose. In the beginning, (voice over Morgan Freeman) God said, "Behold—the egg! Behold—the potato! And my personal favorite, the coffee bean! Choose you this day forward, which will you be?!"

Making choices is always risky. Naturally, most of us don't like too much risk because risk is scary. But it's the only way to grow. We need to jump into that hot pot of boiling water and choose what we're going to be after the water is done with us. It's common to want to be rescued out of the boiling water. But what if the boiling water is what this life is all

about? Reinhold Niebuhr, the author of the Serenity Prayer, sees the boiling water this way: "Accepting hardships as the pathway to peace." What if the boiling water is where our greatest freedom is found?

A Favorite Author I Want You to Know About

Psychiatrist Dr. Viktor Frankl was a prisoner in four Nazi death camps, including Auschwitz, between 1942 and 1945. His parents, brother, and pregnant wife all perished in the horrible extermination of his Jewish countrymen. His experiences are described in the book *Man's Search for Meaning*, with lessons on spiritual survival in the most destitute of circumstances. He writes passionately about humanity's power from a perspective that only deep suffering can produce. "Between stimulus and response there is a space. In that space is our power to choose our response. In our response lies our growth and our freedom." This is one account of Frankl's experience in prison.

> "We who lived in concentration camps can remember the men who walked through the huts comforting others, giving away their last piece of bread. They may have been few in number, but they offer sufficient proof that everything can be taken from a man but one thing: the last of the human freedoms—to choose one's attitude in any given number of circumstances—to choose one's own way.
>
> "And there were always choices to make. Every day, every hour offered the opportunity to make a decision—a decision which determined whether

> you would, or whether you would not submit to the powers which threatened to rob you of your very self, your inner freedom; which determined whether or not you would become the plaything of circumstance, renouncing freedom and dignity to become molded into the form of the typical inmate.[7] It is this spiritual freedom that cannot be taken away, that makes life meaningful and purposeful."[8]

We have the same choice. We may not have the power to dictate how life comes at us or how people behave, but we do have control over how we respond.

The Inmate Inside

When I'm faced with a problem that seems overwhelming, I start to feel powerless and out of options. This powerless feeling spirals me down to a depressed and anxious place that poisons me if I stay there too long. I start feeling trapped between a rock and a hard place. I think, *What is up, God? Why aren't You doing something here?*

This is me in the boiling water. When friends try to help with suggestions, I say "Yeah, but…" and tell them the reasons why nothing will work. This is me being a potato. This is what Frankl recognized as the "typical inmate"—formed and molded by his circumstances to a person with inner powerlessness. I protest (roundly interpreted by those closest to me as "whining"). I grasp for control. I blame. I convince myself that I can't do anything to make myself or

7 Frankl, Viktor E. *Man's Search for Meaning*. New York: Pocket Books, 1984, P.87.

8 Ibid.

my situation better. One day my counselor told me I was acting like a victim. *Oh no, she didn't!* I thought to myself, and drove home mad. The truth can be irritating. This is me being an egg.

Jesus shows us a better way. He came "to proclaim freedom for the prisoners" (Luke 4:18 NIV), because "wherever the Spirit of the Lord is, there is freedom" (2 Corinthians 3:17-18 NLT). "It is for freedom that Christ has set us free. Stand firm, then, and do not let yourselves be burdened again by a yoke of slavery" (Galatians 5:1 NIV).

The inmate inside can yield and be transformed into the free man. The god-figures of the past, or for that matter, the present, see us as slaves, victims or prisoners, but God sees us as free and powerful people. Even in the worst possible situations, people still have a choice of how they will react to it. This act of making a choice in itself is powerful. Spiritual freedoms abound.

"...those who live following the Spirit are thinking about the things the Spirit wants them to do. If people's thinking is controlled by the sinful self, there is death. But if their thinking is controlled by the Spirit, there is life and peace" (Romans 8:5-6 NCV).

Even when the world around us states otherwise, there is an inner reality, an inner freedom that shouts over the static saying, "I am more than what my circumstances dictate to me! I am not defined by other people! I am who God says I am."

Behold, this is me being coffee.

Questions for Self Reflection:

- In what areas of your life do you whine and get soft like the potato?
- In what areas of your life do you feel embittered and hard, like the egg?
- In what areas of your life have you made the choice to turn a problem into an opportunity, like the coffee?
- How have you been an "inmate" inside, and how does that make you feel?
- Write down a small step to help you express your spiritual freedoms.

Intention Statement:

Today I will choose to own my life and the choices I make. I will look for the opportunity in every problem. I will not sulk about my hardships, I will actively engage them, learn from them, and use them to work for me instead of against me.

Extra Study:

Ephesians 5:15-1; Colossians 4:2-6; Galatians 5:1

ten

A Knock off the Old Block

"So God created man in His own image...Then God blessed them..."

Genesis 1:27-28 NKJV

On my 19th birthday, in downtown Ft. Collins, Colorado, I sauntered into an ink parlor and treated myself to a tattoo. Being a little wimpy when it comes to pain, a wild flower the size of a dollar coin was all I was able to tolerate. The tattoo artist got more than a little irritated with my flinching and gave me a firm threat that he wouldn't finish if I didn't suck it up. Suck it up I did, and left happy as a lark once it was all over. Though unaware at the time, that tattoo was part of a grander plan at emancipating myself from childhood restrictions. I still look at it with some pride.

My mother was quietly horrified when I told her. She was quiet about it for days, until finally she said, "That is something your grandmother would have done, too." That is all she had to say. Her mother was loved and respected. She was strong, a non-conformist, and loving. Being told that I was like her in some way was the highest compliment.

There is something special about resembling a respected family member. And why wouldn't I want to be like my grandmother? She was the woman who endured the Depression, raised a family of six in a two bedroom house, and made killer chicken dumplings. She sewed my sister's wedding dress and created oil paintings in her small, crowded bedroom closet. She was the grandma who was hospitalized as a child with a bone disease, raised in the hospital for years apart from her family, and recovered with chronic hip pain and an admirable stubborn streak. She never talked about it, so her private past sufferings raised her to an iconic level. I remember when I was young secretly questioning, "I wonder if I really *could* be like her."

The meaning of *image* is a "reproduction or imitation of the form of a person: a visual representation of someone."[9] Isn't it interesting that we are said to look like, or be in the image of God? It strikes at the same chord. Is it possible that we could really be like God?

How We Were Intended to Be and How We Really Are

In the Garden of Eden, before the onset of human self-reliance, God designed our existence differently than all the other things that He created. We were set apart. The notion made popular by atheistic Darwinists that we are moral animals, but animals nonetheless, is like saying to a child, "There really is nothing special about you."

9 Merriam-Webster, Inc. *Merriam-Webster's Collegiate Dictionary.* Eleventh ed. Springfield, Mass. : Merriam-Webster, Inc., 2003.

But that isn't true. There *is* something special about us. We are god-like. The scripture records God saying to humankind, "You are gods, and all of you are children of the Most High." (Psalm 82:6 NKJV). The word *gods* is likened to "judges" and "mighty ones" in the original language.

God's original creative order is different than what we experience today. People were designed to be blessed, to be successful in deed and relationship to one another. People were created to be stewards and to master the earth. People were created to have authority and power, creativity and ownership, responsibility and security. People were to be kings and queens of the earth, in perfect harmony with one another and with their God. Though the current state of the world is quite different than how originally intended, humankind still bears the marks of divinity.

Each person resembles his Maker, like a daughter resembles her mother, or in my case, a granddaughter resembles her grandmother.

What are the things that you love to do more than anything else? What are the things you do that make you feel most alive, most passionate and in tune with your gifts and talents? Is it when you take photographs, work in the garden, solve problems, write, draw, paint, organize a spreadsheet, teach children, design graphics, drive on the open road, save lives in the ER, perform surgery, argue a case, conduct research, play music, ride horses, decorate interiors, plan events, plan finances, or predict outcomes? When we are in touch with the desires of our hearts and our God-given passions, we are in touch with the very thing that makes us resemble God the most. We taste within ourselves a bit of the Divine.

What it looks like.

On occasion, I have the opportunity to watch my husband in action doing the thing at which he is best: being a leader in his company. I have, of course, seen him in many roles: son-in-law, boyfriend, husband, father, pre-school Sunday School teacher, dog trainer, Air Force officer, and Scrabble champion. I have seen him change diapers, cook dinner, decorate a Christmas tree, drag it out (kicking and cussing), give blood, give money, get embarrassed, get mad, get sick, and gut a deer.

I have witnessed him do all these things and more, but I stand most in awe of him when he is leading his people at work. He motivates, listens, encourages, coaches, and leads with a kind of humble confidence that just makes a person want to be near him. When I get to see it, I see him represent a part of God that I wouldn't have known otherwise or seen anywhere else.

I know a woman who boxed up her dreams of performing music around the time she got married. She had discouraging messages from a high school instructor who profoundly damaged her confidence far beyond graduation, and she eventually stopped believing that she was any good at music at all. A few years after having children, she verbalized her desire to teach them music, and found that the old dream was easily resurrected. As a means of replacing the doubt and shame of the past, she unearthed her old sheet music, researched local theater audition dates, and began to sing again. She no longer denied or quieted the voice of divinity inside of her; instead, she let it out. The little flame that she

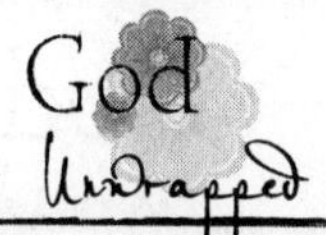

fanned will continue to burn hotter and brighter, bringing light to a formerly dark place.

We are uniquely and masterfully created with great value and worth. But we can easily forget this about ourselves. We seem to have an internal scoreboard of our shortcomings, regrets and insecurities. It is worth our time to unplug from our burden as the scorekeeper and plug into the divinity that God has placed inside of each of us.

Questions for Self Reflection:

- Who are you most like in your family? What passions do you share with this person?
- What God-given desires or assignments do you have?
- How have they changed or stayed the same?
- What divine characteristics within you are underutilized currently?
- What do you do that makes you feel most empowered and alive? What increases your energy, creativity and motivation? These are the things that deserve your focus.
- What activities drain, depress or bore you? These are the things to avoid.

Intention Statement:

Today I will look for God's divine nature in what I do, say, feel, and make. I will validate God's likeness in me and carve out time to prioritize it.

Extra Study:

1 John 3:1; 3 John 11; Ephesians 5:1; Romans 8:21

eleven

Refrigerator God

"The people who don't know God keep trying to get these things, and your Father in heaven knows you need them."

Matthew 6:32 NCV

There was a time when western culture commonly believed only basic needs for food and shelter were necessary for life. This was seen, for example, in the care of children in the 18th and 19th centuries. Before WWII, it was normal for upper society to limit parental time with children to one hour or less a day, thinking that more time would spoil them. Children were regularly separated from their parents for long hospitalizations, boarding school, and foster care arrangements, with little attention being given to the children's sense of loss or possible trauma. Until the 1950s, there was no framework to legitimize other human needs like social and emotional fulfillment. Experimental research like Harry Harlow's on rhesus monkeys and John Bowlby's work on maternal deprivation finally began to change conventional thought.

Now we know that affection and attachment are not only crucial to children's social and cognitive development, but affect their ongoing adult health and well-being, too. But, old habits die hard. The stubborn belief that emotional and social needs are for sissies keeps a lot of so-called "strong" people more like emotional children.

Everyone has unmet needs from their past. Among counseling professionals, that trauma consists of "anything less than nurturing."[10] People who have experienced less than nurturing care from god-figures as they were growing up are likely to have unmet needs and hurts from childhood that creep up on them in marriage, parenting, and work settings. The remedy is recognizing your unmet childhood needs and then finding them in the context of a loving relationship with God and others.

The Adoptive God

We are like an orphaned child adopted by God. A child being introduced into his adoptive home needs some time to adjust and attach with his new caregivers. Healthy attachment must take place in adoptive and foster homes for a child to have the greatest chance of success, so adoptive parents spend a lot of time building rapport and trust to help the child along. The more the child can connect and attach to his new parents, the more successful the transition. The same applies to God. He gets that our god-figures couldn't meet all of our needs, and He makes provision for us within the attachment process to Him.

10 Van der Kolk, Bessel A. MD. "The Psychological Impact of Traumatic Life Experiences." *The Cutting Edge*, January 2008.

Denying Our Needs

The trouble starts when we pretend that our needs really aren't that important. We do to our inner child what was done to us. We tell ourselves, "Well, compared to other people, I didn't have it so bad," or "I shouldn't really feel this way, I should be thankful!" or "I'm fine, I don't need healing." When we deny or minimize our needs, we don't allow Jesus to heal and meet those needs as only He can.

Ryan's Story

Ryan was a 12 year old boy recently adopted by a loving family. Though no one knows exactly what his early years were like, we suspected that he experienced neglect from his caregivers. His parents brought him to counseling because he had a problem with stealing food. He had food in his locker, food in his backpack, food in his pockets and food in his bed. Mom was disgusted, Dad was mad, and the school was threatening suspensions. The more food restrictions there were, the worse the problem got. It turns out that Ryan didn't feel secure unless he had food. A lot of the time, he didn't even eat the food he stole… that's why it rotted in between the sheets of his bed.

We decided to skip the conventional and do something radical. The restrictions were lifted, as was the cap on the school lunch account, and the locks were taken off the refrigerator and pantry door. Mom bought a huge plastic bin and took Ryan grocery shopping to fill it. Together, they bought non-perishable food items that he kept in his room and locker. He could have these items any time he wanted,

as long as he joined them for dinner every night. He could raid the refrigerator, down the orange juice, and drink all the milk. Over time, the stealing, hoarding and hiding of food stopped, as did the constant arguing over food. Ryan felt like he could meet his own needs anytime he needed to—maybe for the first time ever—in the context of a loving home.

God is like "Refrigerator God"—willing and open to meet your needs, whatever they are. He's also the one who gives you the hunger pangs that draw you to Him. He says, "I'll give you what you need, I'll make up for what you didn't get, but have to come to Me to get it." God's refrigerator is stocked with all the things that humans need—not only the things that keep us alive, but the things that keep us well. We may be living, but we're not *really* living unless we meet our needs for love, security, identity, community, and ingenuity at God's refrigerator door.

Figuring Out What Your Needs Are

Discovering and identifying your needs is not always easy. We can agree on the basic needs to survive such as food, shelter and safety. But our emotional needs are often a mystery to be uncovered. Here is a tip: follow your feelings.

Needs for safety: People who have unmet needs for safety, especially in the area of trauma, often will feel fearful when there is no evidence of current danger. You will find that the feelings of fear are anchored in childhood insecurities and past traumatic events. But, you are no longer a child or victim and must convince your heart of this. As a responsible, conscientious adult, you can brainstorm ideas to make yourself feel safe and empowered, i.e. get a dog with a vicious bark, get an alarm system, take a self-defense course, pack heat (within lawful limits, of course), report threatening situations to authorities, etc.

Needs for respect and love: If you feel angry after a discussion with someone at work, then figure out why you are angry. If you felt disrespected, belittled, or ignored, chances are your need for respect was hijacked. If you felt cut off, or unimportant, maybe your need to be heard was bypassed. Let's say that you get depressed when you come home to an empty house. Maybe your need for community and fellowship is underserved. Or maybe it reminds you of your lonely childhood and triggers you to re-experience the wounds of the past. Identifying your feelings and where they are from will help you know how to respond appropriately and receive God's provision for you.

Need for meaningful work: If you feel purposeless, bored, inadequate, or overwhelmed, chances are your self-esteem took a hit somewhere along the line. It was either inflated and spoiled or deflated and ignored—neither option is positive. God has provided meaningful work for you, but embracing it is all up to you. Sometimes you may feel like it's above or beneath you, but His provision is designed to be exactly what you need. Most people find that once they meet other people's needs in the form of meaningful work, they feel satisfied as a result.

> *And my God will meet all your needs according to his glorious riches in Christ Jesus. To our God and Father be glory forever and ever. Amen.*
>
> Philippians 4:19-20 NIV

Questions for Self Reflection:

- How did the god-figures in your life take care of your needs growing up?
- How do you attend to your needs now?
- At first glance, what emotional needs have been denied or minimized in your life? (Common examples are grieving, resting, validation, affection, nurturing, affirmation, attachment, encouragement, and respect.)
- If you had full access to God's refrigerator, what would you consume first?

Intention Statement:

My needs are important and God enables me to meet them in healthy ways. I will look for the ways He wants to meet my needs.

Extra Study:

Exodus 16:16; Matthew 6:31-34; Mark 2:25-28

Twelve

Desire, Demons and Dogs

One spring night, our dog went missing. Spring brings baby rabbits to our neighborhood, and our beagle must have sniffed the flea-infested delights on the breeze, for she quietly sneaked out of the front yard for greater exploits. Once we actually noticed she was gone, my husband valiantly set out in the mini-van to bring her home. While he searched, I conducted my own search of the house, thinking she may be snuggled up somewhere under a bed unbeknownst to us. I did not find our dog, but I did find a stash of wadded up chocolate wrappers carefully hidden inside a large plastic egg under my four-year-old's bed.

Earlier that day, I parceled out some Easter candy to my daughter, which she merrily devoured. But sometime throughout the afternoon, she had found herself wanting, and when her mother said she must wait until after dinner to have any more candy, she took matters into her own hands and swiped the candy, ate the forbidden chocolate, and hid the evidence. The plan could have worked, had it not been for the baby bunnies and the disappearing dog, who, incidentally, returned unharmed and unrepentant.

This is also a human story of getting our needs and desires met by different means than God intended. One of Satan's major functions is to tempt us to meet our needs apart from God. But God knows that our needs will only truly be met by Him, and every other way leaves us worse than when we started. I withheld the candy from my daughter because I knew something she didn't—that too much of the stuff can make a little girl's tummy hurt and can ruin the appetite for healthier fare (plus, she had taken my favorite kind). While I had her best interests in mind, there is another person who does not. Satan has her and all of our moral and eternal destruction in mind. All candy sneaking aside, Satan tempts us to meet our needs and desires in less perfect, ultimately harmful, and even downright evil ways.

Resisting the Quicker, Glitzier, Deadlier

Near the beginning of His ministry, Jesus was led by the Holy Spirit to the wilderness to pray and fast. The Bible says that Satan tempted Jesus in every way while in the wilderness. Jesus can identify with our needs and desires, because He had them too. He also can identify with the strong temptations to meet those needs in quicker, easier, and glitzier ways that are outside of God's plan.

First Satan tempted Jesus to satisfy his hunger by saying, "If You are the Son of God, command that these stones become bread" (Matthew 4:3 NKJV). Hunger is one of humanity's most primal desires, as a need that must be met or death is sure to follow. Satan offered Jesus a way to "cope" with his less-than-desirable circumstances of starvation, homelessness and isolation, by doing things Satan's way.

For us, it may be purchasing a flat screen with a credit card instead of saving up for it. Maybe it's eating a tub of ice cream because you're lonely. It could be not reporting truthfully on your tax return, or looking too long at the pictures on the Internet. Whatever it is, Satan tempts us at our need center, and we are lured to meet our needs in ways that ultimately end in our destruction.

Then, Satan took Jesus into the city and set Him on the highest pinnacle of the temple, and questioned Him again, "If You are the Son of God, throw Yourself down," quoting the scriptures back to Jesus, "'He will order his angels to protect you. And they will hold you up with their hands so you won't even hurt your foot on a stone'" (Matthew 4:6 NLT). Whether Satan was tempting Jesus to commit suicide or to entertain with angel superheroes, I'm not sure. I do know that it was a well-crafted prod to tempt Jesus to question and prove His own identity. Satan was aiming at the epicenter of Jesus' psyche, wanting much more than behavioral allegiance, but also to plant a seed of self-doubt.

Jesus resisted Satan's pressure to minimize Himself or exalt Himself. Later Paul says of Jesus, "He humbled himself and became obedient to death— even death on a cross! Therefore God exalted him to the highest place…" (Philippians 2:8-9 NIV). Though each of us has deep desires to be known, to be recognized, and to be special, we don't have to meet those needs on our own. In fact, the Bible says, "The LORD… lifts up all who are bowed down" (Psalm 145:14 NIV). We are tempted to play down or play up our identities—making ourselves appear pious or powerful, depending on the audience. By waiting on God to lift us up in His appointed time, we bypass the temptation to do it ourselves.

Finally, Satan ups the ante. Almost done, now... just one more shot and this one is aimed at the heart. The scripture says, "Again, the devil took Him up on an exceedingly high mountain, and showed Him all the kingdoms of the world and their glory. And he said to Him, 'All these things I will give You if You will fall down and worship me.'" (Matthew 4:8-9 NKJV). Satan was offering Jesus what was already His, but at a steep price. Satan offers us what is already rightfully ours: love, purpose and power—all the things we deeply long for, but at the cost of our souls. Satan tempts us to go after these things in ways that are quicker, easier, glitzier, and ultimately deadlier than God's ways.

Maybe it's that guy that makes you feel good for the moment, but you know inside that he is taking you down the wrong path. Or could it be stepping in and rescuing someone over and over again, hoping they'll finally change and give you the love you want? In the process of gaining things outside of God's plan for you, you lose the only thing you ever really have—your soul.

Satan tempted Jesus to gain His rightful authority back in ways that were counter to God's best. Because Jesus followed God's best, rejecting any substitute, He transformed the kingdom of the individual heart.

If you know the story, you know that Jesus allowed Satan to tempt Him no further, saying, "Away from me, Satan! For it is written: 'Worship the Lord your God, and serve him only'" (Matthew 4:10 NIV). He was immediately met with God's

total provision for every physical and psychological need. Angels came shortly thereafter, taking care of His needs. He left that place filled with power, comfort, and a greater sense of mission than ever before.

His experience underscores how Satan tempts us to meet our needs in ways counter to God's best. Like Jesus, we can know who we really are without proving it to anyone else. We can withstand and flee from temptation by recognizing and legitimizing our human needs and turning them over to God for provision. We can depend on God to meet our needs, thereby standing against the temptation to get them met in ungodly ways.

Questions for Self Reflection:

- What interaction do you think you have on a daily basis with the tempting of Satan?
- How has this added to your understanding of Satan and his role in the world?
- What did you notice about Jesus' humanity in being tempted?
- What did you notice about Jesus' divinity in being tempted?
- What areas of your own life would you like to have more power over temptation?
- In what ways are you trying to get your needs met in ungodly ways?
- How is God providing for those needs as we speak?

Intention Statement:

He who is in me is greater than he who is in the world. (1 John 4:4)

Extra Study:

1 Corinthians 10:13; James 1:12; 2 Peter 2:9

thirteen

Connecting What's Been Disconnected

"Know that the Lord is God. He made us, and we belong to him; We are his people, the sheep he tends."

Psalm 100:3 NCV

At the 1985 Academy Awards, Sally Field was awarded an Oscar for her performance in the movie "Places of the Heart." While accepting this honor she said, "I've wanted more than anything to have your respect…I can't deny the fact that you like me, right now, you like me!"

Everyone needs to be liked. They need to feel they belong. Brennan Manning, in his book *Ragamuffin Gospel,* describes a scene from an AA meeting that describes this need well:

> "On a sweltering summer night in New Orleans, sixteen recovering alcoholics and drug addicts gather for their weekly AA meeting. Although several members attend other meetings during the week, this is their home group. They have been meeting on Tuesday nights for several years and know each

> other well. Some talk to each other daily on the telephone and others socialize outside the meetings. Their personal investment in one another's sobriety is sizable. Nobody fools anybody else. Everyone is there because he or she made a slobbering mess of his or her life and is trying to put the pieces back together. Each meeting is marked by levity and seriousness. Some members are wealthy, others middle class, or poor. Some smoke, others don't. Most drink coffee. Some have graduate degrees, others have not finished high school. For one small hour the high and mighty descend and the lowly rise. The result is fellowship."[11]

Fellowship is essential to growth and health. God made Eve for Adam, Jonathan for David, Mary for Martha, John for Jesus, Ruth for Billy, and Tom for Jerry. God made us to need each other. God made it so that life would only work well in relationship with other people. They grow us up, weed us out and talk us down. Each relationship has the capacity to hurt and to heal, sometimes all in a day. Jesus knew we needed people, and repeatedly emphasized our living in community with one another.

Jesus himself instigated the same sub-cultural mixers as the AA meeting. Jesus brought people together, and purposely spiced things up in a very sterile and classist culture. There once was a wealthy tax collector named Zacchaeus who made his fortune by collecting more than the state's share of taxes from the common people. Tax collectors were roundly despised, thought of with ill repute, and sneered at as sinners.

11 Manning, Brennan. *Ragamuffin Gospel.* Sisters, Oregon: Multnoma Publishers, 2000, P. 66.

To top it off, Zacchaeus was very short—children sing about his diminished stature still today.

One day, Jesus made his debut in Zacchaeus' hometown of Jericho and drew a crowd of people, as usual. The wee little wealthy man had to climb a sycamore tree just to get a good glimpse of Jesus. Though he was tucked away amongst the tree limbs, Jesus spotted him like a hunter, and called, "Zacchaeus, hurry and come down! I must stay at your house today" (Luke 19:5).

The laws that were in place that protected the "clean" from the "unclean" were so stringent, that just going into Zacchaeus' home would be considered sinful. Zacchaeus never would have had the courage to invite a rabbi to dinner, knowing that his offer would be rejected. So, Jesus invited Himself. The crowd was aghast! What was Jesus doing socializing with this tax collecting swindler? Unruffled by the crowd's opinion, Zacchaeus excitedly shimmied down that tree and gladly met Jesus with a change of heart. Zacchaeus committed to give back what he had taken from the people and to give what he owned to the poor.

But the story doesn't end with Zacchaeus and Jesus walking off into the sunset. Like spreading icing on the baklava, Jesus turns to the crowd to publicly reinstate Zacchaeus to his rightful place in the community by saying, "Salvation has come to this house today, this man also belongs to the family of Abraham." Jesus was concerned with re-introducing a man who had once been culturally blacklisted into the right standing of society.

Jesus understands our need to be loved and to belong.

Some of us just need to know that the need to belong is legitimate. It is ok to want to belong. It is ok to want to fit. Zacchaeus not only needed the community around him, but *they* needed Zacchaeus.

Things that Keep People from Belonging

Fear of rejection. Because people are unsure that they are truly acceptable and lovable, they fear that others will reject them and confirm what they've feared all along. They keep their authentic selves hidden from view and reap superficial relationships with others. By taking small risks and sharing your heart, dreams, and disappointments with caring people, you will gain social confidence.

Lacking social skills. Some folks haven't learned appropriate skills modeled by healthy people, so they don't know what makes up a healthy relationship. Let's take Zacchaeus for example. What if his size was a source of shame that festered into malicious arrogance and thievery? What if he never learned to accept himself in relation to other people because other people never took him seriously? The only way he felt like he could gain others' respect was to make them fear him. Jesus offered him acceptance and respect, enabling him to accept and respect himself. Relational skills can be learned through trusted mentors, counselors, and friends. These skills will attract healthy people who offer real love and belonging.

Attracting unhealthy people. I've heard this trait described as having a "broken people-picker." People tend to be drawn to the familiar, even if it's "unhealthy familiar" and will repeat the patterns of the past. We fear being vulnerable and truly

known to the point of self-sabotage—choosing people who will reenact the patterns of rejection, dependence, and pain of the past. Inviting feedback from trusted individuals like a counselor, pastor, or mentor can be very helpful in learning how to pick healthy people with whom to share life.

Habits and addictions. Ranging from working too many hours to escaping through substances, addictions isolate people from authentic loving relationships. People who struggle with addictive activities hide their true selves behind the addictive behaviors, keeping them from receiving love and belonging from others. They find themselves in a never ending cycle of shame, defeat, and hopelessness. More often than not, addicted people received little unconditional positive regard from the god-figures in their lives and are unfamiliar with anything other than deadening their pain with the addiction. A strong, consistent support system committed to recovery and the reclaiming of the spiritual self is needed.

God never designed us to be alone, self-sufficient, or cut off from loving relationships. Healthy relationships play an essential role in healing the soul. Little transformation can happen without healthy bonding with other people. God designed us to engage with others in an authentic way, accepting others with their shortcomings as they accept us, and then encouraging one another to press on toward Christ-likeness. God desires us to be not only restored to Him, but to be restored to people.

Questions for Self Reflection:

- How did you experience love and belonging growing up?
- What love and belonging needs remain unmet?
- In what areas of your life would you like to experience God's provision for your need of love and belonging?
- What first step will you take to receive this provision?

Intention Statement:

I will commit to entering and maintaining healthy relationships with others.

Extra Study:

Hebrews 10:24-25; 1 Corinthians 14:26;
1 John 4:12; Galatians 5:13

fourteen
The Great Cover-Up

"So she took some of the fruit and ate it. Then she gave some to her husband, who was with her, and he ate it, too. At that moment their eyes were opened, and they suddenly felt shame at their nakedness."

Genesis 3:6-7 NLT

I remember the day when I noticed my daughter, who was somewhere between two and three years old, first experiencing shame. For such a long time, she did not know what shame was. She dribbled and drooled on herself, she made embarrassing noises, she wobbled and fell down when trying to walk, but none of these things produced shame in her until that day. She pronounced a word in the cutest way imaginable, and I smiled with delight in the pleasure of hearing it. But she was not so delighted. She turned red, and said, "Not funny!" She was aware that she mispronounced the word. My smile, though innocent, registered to her that I was laughing at her mistake. I don't know when she became conscious that it was embarrassing to mispronounce a word, but there it was, written all over her face. Then she buried her head and cried. I cried too, because it was the end of innocence for her.

Up until that point she could explore, fall down, make mistakes, be messy, get things wrong, and still feel ok about herself. Her innocent failings did not affect what she thought about herself, because they were not failings to her, they were "tryings." That day she was aware of her failed attempts, her inabilities, her feelings of being "less than," and she was ashamed of it. She wanted to disappear.

Psychoanalyst Erik Erickson is known for mapping human development from cradle to grave. Children between the ages of 18 months and 3 years are in the developmental stage called Autonomy vs. Shame and Doubt. During this stage, the child must accomplish a few tasks of independence like potty training and feeding himself to develop an appropriate sense of self will. A toddler expressing his own will, even when he says "No" to his mother is a good thing, because it means that he is separating himself from his mother and becoming his own person. If this budding independence is not allowed or nurtured in a productive way, or if it is scolded harshly and shamed, then the child will feel shame for becoming his own person, as if there is something innately wrong with him being who he really is.

Shame is a normal and natural emotion that we all possess. It comes when we do something wrong, embarrassing, or something just *perceived* as wrong and embarrassing. People say things like, "I just wanted to disappear," or "I could have just died!" My mom and I are the lucky recipients of the red-face gene when we get embarrassed. At the precise moment we'd like to become invisible, we turn neon red. It's just great. Then all socially inept people around us seem compelled to call more attention to us by pointing and saying, "Oh, you're

turning red!" Thank you, thanks for mentioning that. That really helps.

After I had heard what my daughter said, she and I hugged, and I affirmed that she was bright and enjoyable and brave for trying, and that I smile at her because I am happy when I am with her. I told her that when she was ready, we would practice the word together. She was ashamed of her own ability, but I was not ashamed of her. Though she was soothed for the moment, I was aware that she had joined the human race in experiencing shame, and that she would never enjoy pure and sustained shamelessness until the other side of glory.

Original Sin

The Garden of Eden was the original design, where God placed Adam and Eve with access to resources that would meet their every need. They experienced the absence of anything negative or painful and the presence of everything pleasant and sweet, until they broke from His original design. They chose to meet their needs apart from God and against the plan.

The Un-doer of everything good slithered in as a snake and convinced Eve that God was trying to pull one over on her. It's kind of like how my daughter thought I was laughing at her when she mispronounced the word. No one likes to be kept in the dark about something—no one likes to be played the fool. Eve began to believe that God was just trying to control her and keep her down.

Little did she know that once she and Adam took the bite of the forbidden fruit, the consequence of the sin was born *in* her and the immediate feeling she experienced was not power that comes from knowledge. It was not wisdom that leads to goodness. It was shame...the kind of shame that makes a person want to disappear forever...the kind of shame that makes a person doubt who she is...the kind of shame that drives her to isolate herself from the One who loves her. And so began the Great Cover-Up. The biblical account says,

> At that moment their eyes were opened, and they suddenly felt shame at their nakedness. And they heard the sound of the LORD God walking in the garden in the cool of the day, and Adam and his wife hid themselves from the presence of the LORD God among the trees of the garden.
>
> Then the LORD God called to Adam and said to him, "Where *are* you?"
>
> So he said, "I heard Your voice in the garden, and I was afraid because I was naked; and I hid myself."
>
> And He said, "Who told you that you were naked? Have you eaten from the tree of which I commanded you that you should not eat?" (Genesis 3:7-13 NKJV)

Their nakedness was beautiful and perfect and meant for delight and satisfaction. They were meant to enjoy their own perfectly created body and to enjoy the other's perfectly created body. They were to live in the garden and rule the garden and everything in it. Their nakedness had always meant joyful freedom in themselves and freedom in pleasure.

Take, for example, the beauty of the woman, created as an expression of God's own beauty, stunning the created world with her extravagantly gorgeous naked self—until sin entered the scenario, and then her nakedness meant shamefulness. How demoralizing and sad!

Today, the cosmetic surgery business is booming to nip and tuck that shameful thing to a more presentable state. Girdles, miracle bras, enhancers, padding, makeup, botox, cosmetic dentistry—just think of all the ways women work to hide the real self. Shame is good for business!

Shame was the immediate result of sinning against God, and with it a knowledge and abhorrence of who we really are. My daughter, because of Adam and Eve's spiritual genetic legacy, inherited the knowledge that she is a shameful person, and that who she is should be covered up, hidden, denied, rejected and ruminated over, if ever a mistake or imperfection leaks out.

We have the sinking feeling that there is something innately wrong with us, and we are right.

The moment Adam and Eve knew they sinned, they went to work sewing fig leaves to cover themselves. Similarly, we create temporary solutions to cover our sin, like perfectionism, blame-shifting, projecting, denial, and numbing.

But God made a solution that doesn't end in self-destruction. "And the LORD God made clothing from animal skins for Adam and his wife" (Genesis 3:21 NLT). This was the first time the shedding of innocent blood was used to cover human shame. God made provision through the blood

of an animal to cover both the beauty *and* the shame of our nakedness. Our bodies were no longer beautiful houses for glory, they were prisons from our freedom. The blood of the animal was symbolic for us—something died so we could live. Freedom can only be won through sacrifice.

Grace Land

Since that time, the ultimate Sacrifice was given. God himself sacrificed His life to cover our shame and set us free through Christ's death and resurrection. We now live in a new age. It's called the "age of grace." I like to call it my promise land. In reality, I live in God's gracious freedoms all the time—the freedom to be who I really am, the freedom to fall short and still be loved, and the freedom to make my own choices. I have tasted my promise land and it tastes good! It's full of life and growing things and liberality and dreams and sufficiency and opportunity. I see everything in the light of God's love—the joyful and the painful things. I love it there—it's my Eden.

But sometimes I wander away from home. I get distracted, hell bent, caught up, and thrown off course. All of a sudden I look around and I find myself in the desert. I see the promise land far away and I'd like to go back. But I stay right there in the wilderness, full of doubt, lacking in purpose and feeling angry at myself for losing my way. Sometimes, I even let myself get hauled back into slavery in Egypt, letting other people dictate to me who I am and what I'm good for. When I come to my senses, I say to myself, "How could I leave the freedom I had? Why do I toil and strive and stress, when there is rest back home?"

Then I hear God call my name, "Michelle, where are you?" I let Him see my silly attempt to cover myself with leaves. He says, "Have you strayed, leaving your home with Me, to put yourself in the desert again?"

He picks me up, brushes me off and affirms me by saying, "You are bright and you are enjoyable and you are brave for trying, and I smile at you because I like to be with you. And when you are ready, we will walk back to the promise land together. You are ashamed of yourself, but I am not ashamed of you." He takes away the leaves and covers me in Christ. There's no groveling or begging or promises to do it right next time. There's just the embrace, and the embrace is enough to start again.

How to Un-Cover and Heal

1) Name the embarrassing events in your past, being careful to identify who, what, and when.

2) Be your own best friend and go back in your mind and make it right. For instance, tell your inner child that he's just human and normal and prone to mistakes. Imagine confronting the shaming event with mercy. Let your shamed self off the hook by accepting the part of yourself that feels too shameful to be accepted.

3) Say what needs to be said.

4) Forgive those who have shamed, embarrassed or belittled you in the past.

5) Commit to a process of self-acceptance.

Questions for Self Reflection:

- What memories of your childhood cause embarrassment?
- What areas of your life do you feel embarrassed about now (status, appearance, possessions, your children's behavior, etc)?
- Have you experienced living in the promise land with God?
- In what areas of your life are you still wandering in the desert?
- What would it be like to believe that God is not ashamed of you?
- In what areas of your life would you like to live in greater freedom and grace?

Intention Statement:

Today I receive God's grace in place of my shame. I will not only believe that I am acceptable before God, I will also accept myself.

Extra Study:

Hebrews 12:2; 1 John 2:28 to 1 John 3:3

fifteen

"I Do"

"For if we live, we live to the Lord; and if we die, we die to the Lord. Therefore, whether we live or die, we are the Lord's."

Romans 14:8 NKJV

When my husband and I got married, it was popular to write your own vows. I tried, but I couldn't come up with anything that didn't sound cheesy. My husband is a guy's guy, and I could just imagine presenting my home-crafted lines, "Oh, Love of all loves, and Man of all men, You light up my life, and make me want to sin …." And him at the altar trying not to bust the button on his tux by keeping in the laughter. So we settled on the traditional vows.

"Will you, Michelle, have Brian to be your husband? Will you love him, comfort and keep him, and forsaking all others remain true to him as long as you both shall live?" ("I do.") "With this ring I thee wed, and all my worldly goods I thee endow. In sickness and in health, in poverty or in wealth, 'til death do us part." Once the marriage commences, these vows may make us *wish* for an early death, but the vows remain the same. Some vows are humanly impossible to keep. A promise broken, a sin unforgiven, and a relationship ruined. This is common in human relationships, but not so with God. Leaving His lover is unimaginable.

The Song of Solomon is widely known as a book of lovers. The young woman in the love affair praises her man for all his attributes of strength and beauty. She pursues him, looks for him, and is full of joy when she finds him. The groom returns these praises by describing her beauty in poetic prose. He goes so far as to describe every part of her body—her eyes, teeth, lips, hair, neck, breasts, navel, and feet. I may suggest that Brian write his own poem, maybe about my feet—I'm sure he would have some material to work with. By the scripture written, we know that the young woman is completely naked before him, and he says to her, "All beautiful you are, my darling; there is no flaw in you" (Song of Solomon 4:7 NIV).

But how do people feel when the true self is really exposed? Pretty self conscious, right? Rarely will a client feel completely comfortable when they talk about private feelings in my office. Even among friends, we experience some stress and discomfort when we open up. Being authentic, real, and exposed makes us vulnerable. It's hard to do.

But the Bible instructs us to, "come boldly to the throne of our gracious God. There we will receive his mercy, and we will find grace to help us when we need it most" (Hebrews 4:16 NLT). The *Message Bible* paraphrases the same verse as, "So let's walk right up to him and get what he is so ready to give. Take the mercy, accept the help."

We can come to God the same way the young woman came to her lover. She was uncovered and not ashamed. Because of the intense love that the young man had for his bride, he overlooked any flaw, birthmark, tan line, stray hair, sweat smell, stretch mark, pimple, bulge, or scar. Jesus' "love will cover a multitude of sins" (1 Peter 4:7-8 NKJV) and trouble areas. Jesus reassures us that He sees us through the eyes of love. He is not like the other god-figures in our lives. He doesn't take the opportunity to leave us, criticize us or look the other way when we open ourselves up to Him. He stays through sickness and in health, poverty and wealth, layoffs and promotions, start-ups and bankrupts, stupidity and wisdom, craziness and sanity, sagginess and hormones, (hey, I think I've finally written my own vows!).

We ask ourselves, "Am I good enough to be loved? Am I acceptable just the way that I am?" But maybe these are the wrong questions. Maybe the better question is, "Is God good enough to love me, no matter what?" This takes the pressure off of our performance, and puts it on His.

Our acceptability has little to do with us and everything to do with how good God is and how perfect Jesus' sacrifice is. "For God's will was for us to be made holy by the sacrifice of the body of Jesus Christ, once for all time" (Hebrews 10:10 NLT) and, "for by that one offering he forever made perfect those who are being made holy" (Hebrews 10:14 NLT).

We are acceptable because God says so, and when God says, "I do," that vow is so solid and tight, it is unbreakable. That means that nothing we can do would make us more or less perfect to Him. As we come in love to Jesus, He overlooks the flaws.

Saying "I Do" to Yourself

Once you've warmed to the idea that God is not going anywhere, you may need to extend the same grace to yourself. *Splitting* is a process of denying parts of our authentic self in order to be seen as acceptable. People have a way of unconsciously denying, hiding or suppressing valid and valuable parts of themselves for fear of being rejected, humiliated or manipulated. For example, let's imagine that I have a "quick wit" that has gotten me into trouble in the past. I could wish that I was nicer, or sweeter or quieter because that is the appropriate thing for a Christian woman to be. I could try to suppress it, hide it or starve it to be more acceptable.

But the better way is, instead of shaming Quick-wit into silence, I make sure she's fed, tamed and put on a leash. Then I can use her as necessary, like the time the weirdo in the grocery store was gawking at my daughters and following them around. Quick-wit and her counterpart Mean-streak barked up a storm and Weirdo high tailed it out of there.

My job is to boldly bring all the parts together before God: Mean-streak, Nincompoop, Quick-wit, Potty-mouth, Sad-sack, and the good ones too . As I humbly expose my true self to God, I can receive love from Him in every part of me. This allows Him to integrate those parts to make me a whole, well-loved person.

Turn the vows to yourself, "I will love, comfort and keep you, remaining true to you as long as I live. In sickness, health, poverty or wealth, forsaking all temptations to do otherwise till death unites me fully with Christ."

Questions for Self Reflection:

- Is there anything that keeps you from coming to God, like the bride in Song of Solomon came to the bridegroom?
- Do you believe that God sees you as all beautiful and flawless?
- Have you "exposed" yourself to other god-figures that have been less than accepting? How has that affected you? If you were to really accept yourself with all the known imperfections, what would it mean for your life?
- What parts of yourself do you split off?

Intention Statement:

Today I will act as if God sees me through His intense love. Today I will act as if I am the lovable, acceptable person God has made me to be.

Extra Study:

Hebrews 4:12-16; Hebrews 5:9; Ephesians 4:13

sixteen

The Masterpiece and His Master

"But I am like an olive tree, growing in God's Temple. I trust God's love forever and ever."

Psalm 52:8-9 NCV

A few years ago, I visited Florence, Italy and saw Michelangelo's "David. " The statue, completed in 1504, stands 17 feet high, and is breathtaking. The information I found to be most intriguing (no, not just that he is naked), was regarding the block of marble Michelangelo used. It was originally from a quarry in Carrara, a town in the Italian Alps. After a few attempts by other artists, it remained neglected for twenty-five years, all the while exposed to the elements in the yard of the cathedral workshop. The elements weathered it, and the Operai (a group who commissioned artists for work), was determined to find an artist who could take this expensive, rare piece of marble and turn it into a finished work of art. Though Leonardo da Vinci and others were consulted, it was young Michelangelo, only twenty-six years old, who convinced the Operai that he deserved the commission.

On August 16, 1501, Michelangelo was given the official contract to undertake this challenging new task. He worked on the massive biblical hero for a little more than three years. It is speculated that although other artists gave the marble a try, it was only Michelangelo who envisioned David in the marble and could bring him into reality.

God is our master-craftsman. He, like Michelangelo, sees us as the finished product already. Within the uncut marble, He sees a masterpiece. The marble has been worn and diminished by years of exposure, and has been started and left unfinished by other artisans—artisans who didn't have the same vision in mind. But the Master Craftsman eagerly jumps to work when He sees it. He works with joy at chipping away the useless bits until He can see the round cheek bones of the face. He rounds out the rough edges until the gentleness of the neck can be plainly seen. He hammers out the proverbial chips on the shoulders until He can see the strength of stature. He carves deeply into the hard stone with power and precision. He perfects the hands for working and the feet for walking and the heart for loving, all the while seeing us as we were originally intended to be—without sin, without the Fall, and totally whole. He sees us exactly like He sees His Son, Jesus.

God gets that we are human. No matter how human we are, He sees us as His children. His love for us is so intense that He keeps in His mind a picture of who we really are. It is the Father's *love* for us that continues to hold the vision for our good and best, even when we have fallen short, and maybe even moved far off course.

In Christ, we have already been made whole, perfect and complete. Paul writes, "Now to Him who is able to do exceedingly abundantly above all that we ask or think, according to the power that works in us, to Him be glory..." (Ephesians 3:20-21 NKJV). It is God's hand that is perfecting us, not our own, and He is able to accomplish the work that He has started. Paul also writes, " He will take our weak mortal bodies and change them into glorious bodies like his own" (Philippians 3:21 NLT).

I believe that Paul was a lot like us, and like any truth-telling person, had doubts about himself, his life, his growth (or lack thereof), his purpose, and his worth. If he didn't, he wouldn't be human. The admirable quality of Paul is that he came out on the other side of his darkness with true and tested claims of faith that God would finish what he started. Paul says, "I know Jesus, the One in whom I have believed. And I am sure he is able to protect what he has trusted me with until that day" (2 Timothy 1:12 NCV).

If we could really see ourselves in the spiritual realm exactly the way God sees us, we wouldn't see ourselves as sinners saved by grace, we would see ourselves as saints who sometimes sin. [12] We'd see ourselves as the masterpiece that is in the process of being perfected. Take a look at the comparative tables on the next page.

12 I heard Pete Briscoe preach this in his church, Bent Tree Bible Fellowship, one Sunday—an enlightening view regarding our position in Christ.

Seeing Ourselves as Saints	Seeing Ourselves as Sinners
• Being good enough. • Being perfected in Christ-likeness at the initiation and finishing of God's hand. • Accept self and be empowered as a master over religious expectations. • Accept and love others where they are on their own life journey. • Weakness is not an *indictment* against the self, it is an *opportunity* for God's strength. • Join with God as a fellow worker in the growth process and Kingdom of God. • Collaborate with others in a common mission and goal.	• Flawed, unable to ever measure up. • Heaven bound, but doomed for failure. • Frustrated with self and impossible religious expectations. • Compare self to others resulting in judgment or jealousy. • When weak, we motivate ourselves with guilt, and call it "conviction from God." • Perform for God, hoping to please Him. • Compete with others for social, economic or religious "ranking"

The Bible talks a lot about the believer being perfected and made holy. Paul, in the New Testament, writes about presenting "every man perfect in Christ Jesus" (Colossians 1:28 NKJV). Another scripture describes being "perfect in Christ" this way: "efficient and graceful in response to God's Son, fully mature adults, fully developed within and without, fully alive like Christ. No prolonged infancies among us, please… God wants us to grow up…like Christ in everything" (Ephesians 4:13-15 MSG).

Believers are in the process of being perfected. A useful definition of *perfect* is being thoroughly complete or whole; like a finished masterpiece. Our only part in this process of perfection is being yielded to the Master's hands. When we are focused on God's work in us, instead of our work for Him, the pressure of *being perfect* is replaced with the promise of *being perfected*. The pressure is on the Master Artisan, not on the lump of beloved marble.

Questions for Self Reflection:

- Do you believe that your sinful nature affects the way God sees you?
- Does God see you as a sinner (bad) or as a child (loved)?
- What parts of your "marble" is God carving, chiseling, and smoothing out?

Intention Statement:

My growth is less about me trying,
and more about God perfecting.

Extra Study:

Romans 3:31; Romans 4:19; Galatians 3:1-7

seventeen

The Smeagol Inside

"You, my brothers, were called to be free. But do not use your freedom to indulge the sinful nature; rather, serve one another in love. The entire law is summed up in a single command: 'Love your neighbor as yourself.' If you keep on biting and devouring each other, watch out or you will be destroyed by each other."

Galatians 5:13-15 NIV

The character Smeagol in J.R.R. Tolkien's trilogy "Lord of the Rings" is an irresistible symbol of powerlessness and carnality. Smeagol, and his alter personality, Gallum, is a small, repulsive fellow given to selfish lusts. He is confused, self-loathing and simultaneously self-serving. Smeagol's one desire is to possess the powerful Ring that would give him everything he could ever want, but his desire ultimately enslaves him, making him utterly powerless. He says, "We wants it, we needs it. Must have the precious. They stole it from us. Sneaky little hobbitses. Wicked, tricksy, false!"

Smeagol is a great word picture for what the Bible calls, "the flesh." The flesh is concerned with getting its own way, and not having the capacity to think beyond the desire. I think of "flesh" as akin to the Freudian term "id." You may remember from Psych 101 that Freud's id was described as an instinctual drive, always striving toward satisfying primal needs for pleasure. Like a two year old that is unable to think rationally or morally, the id is only aware of what he wants and how can he get it. Jesus mentions the Smeagol-type flesh when He instructs His sleepy disciples to pray in the garden of Gethsemane. He said, "Watch and pray, lest you enter into temptation. The spirit indeed is willing, but the flesh is weak" (Mark 14:38 NKJV). The disciples' desire for sleep, for example, was not bad, it just wasn't best. Or better put, fully grown. Smeagol started out as a nice little hobbit, until his desire was un-tethered from maturity. Had his desire and pleasure been tempered with love and self-control, his life could have matured. But as it was, his primal and solitary drive for pleasure resulted in jealousy to the point of murder.

The Smeagol Inside

There is a similar story in the Bible about the First Family, and coincidentally, the first homicide. Cain and Abel were brothers. Both were born with the Smeagol inside, but only one of them allowed himself to be *ruled* by it.

Abel brought an offering of his best sheep to God, and God accepted it. Cain brought his own offering but it wasn't his best and God wasn't pleased with it. The Bible, in the book of Leviticus, goes into great detail to describe what kind of offering is acceptable and what kind isn't. It says, "When

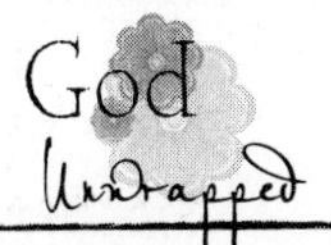

a man offers a sacrifice... it must be perfect to be accepted; there shall be no defect in it" (Leviticus 22:20-21 NASB). A perfect gift is always from a heart of love.

Cain was enraged. He fumed, and festered, and thought of the unthinkable.[13] God interrupted Cain's adult-sized tantrum and said, "Why are you angry? Why is your face downcast? If you do what is right, will you not be accepted? But if you do not do what is right, sin is crouching at your door; it desires to have you, but you must master it" (Genesis 4:6-7 NIV).

God reminded Cain that he had the power over the Smeagol inside to make things right. His fragile self-esteem was so wounded that he could not control his jealousy over Abel's success. He who was created to rule, was ruled and powerless over his selfish lust for revenge. Cain invited his brother Abel out into the field, where Cain killed him in cold blood and was later banished from the land for life.

We all have passion, drive, emotion, and desires—these are not bad, wrong or evil. Unmanaged, however, they can turn into sin, addictions and idolatry. It is our *human destiny* to master the Smeagol inside. God interrupts our desires with His Spirit and offers space to make a choice: to either master them or be mastered by them. Mastering them means power. Being mastered by them means slavery. To master them means:

- I may throw myself a pity party but I'll leave before midnight.

13 Note, God was the recipient of the "not so nice gift", but Cain was mad.... Pretty backwards, don't you think?

- I may get angry and jealous, but I won't satisfy those emotions with gossip or revenge.
- I may get hurt, but I won't hurt back.
- I have strong desires, but they serve a strong Spirit.
- I may have been victimized, but I am not a victim.
- I may lament that life is hard, but I can do hard things through Christ's strength.
- My desires, feelings, and passions are knelt down before my greater purpose.

Let's take Cain as an example again and play out "what could have been." What if Cain had reacted differently? Let's give him permission to still get mad, rant and rave, and generally feel inferior and rejected. Then, after sufficient time in his tantrum, God pursues him, asking why he's angry. But this time, Cain responds to God by opening up all those feelings. Maybe he would say something like, "Abel is always so perfect! Mom and Dad always favored him, and now You're favoring him! He can't do anything wrong. And I'm always the screw up!"

Then maybe God would say something like, "I understand how you feel. I've seen everything that's gone on in your family. But don't let that get to you. Don't try to out-do your brother. Just do what is right. Give from your heart, not from competition. Once you do that, it doesn't matter what they do, you'll have My acceptance."

Then maybe Cain would come around, and say, "God, You're right. I gave my offering for the wrong reasons. I'm not going to take my frustration out on Abel. This is between You and me, I don't have to worry about them. Say, God, I had this really good idea for my next offering… what do You think about…." And then Cain's desire would be energized again, but course-corrected back into the flow of God's Spirit. In addition, as Cain matures through practice, he will have a quicker turn-around time. He may be triggered by feelings of inferiority in the future, but because he's made a practice of turning those feelings over to God, he'll get back on track long before murder ever crosses his mind. I can see a bright future for this Cain!

The Bible says, "The one who sows to please his sinful nature, from that nature will reap destruction; the one who sows to please the Spirit, from the Spirit will reap eternal life" (Galatians 6:8 NIV). We have all been called to a life of freedom in Christ, but to use that freedom in order to satisfy the flesh is to our own demise. Bringing our desires under submission to the Spirit is the ultimate in power because we then have the force of our desire to fuel our greater purpose.

Questions for Self Reflection:

- What desires are the hardest to master? They may be found at the core of your deepest disappointments.
- When has your desire turned into a sin and mastered you?
- How have you given up your power in the past?
- What spiritual choices do you have right now? How will you feed the flesh or feed the Spirit?
- What attitude will you choose toward making yourself spiritually free and strong?
- When do you feel like a powerful person?

Intention Statement:

Today I will take charge of my life by taking responsibility for my actions as well as seeking opportunities to grow and to temper my desires in submission to God.

Extra Study:

Galatians 6:4-5; Romans 8:1-2, 6-7

eighteen
Love's Substitutes

"And I pray that you and all God's holy people will have the power to understand the greatness of Christ's love..."

Ephesians 3:18 NCV

I have succumbed to the bliss of a pre-lit imitation Christmas tree. It is truly sublime. My tree waits for me in the rafters of the garage, patiently, quietly, until the day after Thanksgiving, when its branches can unfurl and twinkle and sit perfectly upon one another at just the right angle. Oh, there were real trees before it, but none were as perfect as the imitation tree I have now. No more dry needles, no more watering the trunk, no more traipsing through the aisles of street tree markets, or worse—foraging in the mean, cold, sasquatch-infested woods of the Northwest. And I don't even have to miss the smell of the real tree because they make an imitation evergreen spray! Oh the joy of imitation!

Until... one little twinkling light goes on the fritz and affects the whole string of twinkling lights, and try as I might, I am unable to find the one blasted light that's out. Bliss is replaced with rage and threats and words best left bleeped. And then the kids start complaining that they can't even *remember* a time that they had a *real* tree, and how sad it is to be children in the Hollomon house where the imitation is celebrated above authenticity! That does it. If they can prove philosophically that there is a moral issue at stake, I am putty in their hands. And off to the woods we go: bear spray in hand, just in case, proudly choosing the higher moral road of cutting down a real tree for Christmas!

Ok, honestly speaking, it does feel a bit like cheating when I pull that imitation tree out of its box, set it up, and plug it in… all under 5 minutes. It looks pretty perfect, but I am missing the *process* of the Christmas tree. Christmas trees aside, maybe it's the process of life God cares about, not perfection and ease. Maybe it's the *real* God wants, and not the *ideal.*

Many have chosen imitation love over the real thing. Maybe we settle for it because it looks real and it smells real, and we just *want* it to be real. This is especially true when we settle for religion over relationship. I've done it, and you've probably done it. It's like sugar substitute—it tastes sweet enough but it leaves a bad aftertaste and our craving for the real thing is still there. Our substitutes have the appearance of love, but have no transformational qualities. God refuses to let us be satisfied with the imitation. He doesn't just want us to look real, he wants us to *be* real.

Sarah's Story

Sarah and her family belonged to a small church in a small town. She described a fellowship where all of the families "looked" the same, raised their families the same, chose the same method of educating their children, same gender role delineation, and the same method of moderating their children's dating. The church was caught up in a system of sub-cultural rules and regulations. Some were spoken, some were not. Difference was not tolerated, and outsiders were not welcome.

This kind of church isn't uncommon. John Ortberg said, "Groups have a tendency to be exclusive. Insiders want to separate themselves from outsiders. So they adopt boundary markers. These are highly visible, relatively superficial practices...whose purpose is to distinguish between those inside a group and those who are outside." He goes on to say, "What's worse, the insiders become proud and judgmental toward outsiders."[14] The sub-cultural norms of Sarah's church were used to identify not only if you belonged, but how holy you were—or at least how holy you appeared. The group's love and acceptance was based on and earned by adherence to rules and moral behavior, and fed by fear of rejection and chastisement.

Other groups may have other sub-cultural ways to determine how acceptable you are, like the part of town where you live, the type of car that you drive, the style of jeans that you wear, whether your kids go to public or private school, if you're a white collar or blue collar worker, a working or stay-at-home mom, if your car is a hybrid or a gas guzzler, and on and on. Sarah's group was concerned with holiness, while other groups are concerned with success or education or

---

14 Ortberg, John. *The Life You've Always Wanted.* Grand Rapids, Michigan: Zondervan, 1997, p. 31, 32.

looks or a certain brand of activism. These group distinctions can be the most hurtful when they're found in the Christian church. When you feel like an outsider in church, the rejection is compounded.

After 10 years, Sarah and her husband began to challenge a few of these unspoken rules in their circle of friends. Not long after, they were ratted out and decisively rubbed out of church membership. Some of the elders went so far as prophesying curses over her family if they didn't repent. Trips to the local supermarket invited cold shoulders and snubbed noses from people they thought were their friends.

After the initial shock of excommunication, the loss of the perceived closeness sank in. Sarah grieved the loss of the people she thought were friends. She grieved the church she thought was her family. She thought they were close. But what she had with them was a false intimacy, not true love and friendship. It was based on superficial appearances and performance. Once Sarah could see clearly, she could see her church for the imitation it really was. Jesus said "What sorrow awaits you teachers of religious law and you Pharisees. Hypocrites! For you are like whitewashed tombs—beautiful on the outside but filled on the inside with dead people's bones and all sorts of impurity. Outwardly you look like righteous people, but inwardly your hearts are filled with hypocrisy and lawlessness" (Matthew 23:27-28 NLT).

In the midst of Sarah's loneliness, God showed up. Unshackled from the religiosity, she was free to discover a very different God. She said, "Until now, I don't think I ever really knew about God's love—and I mean God's love for *me.*" And how could she? There was so much other stuff in the way. After a stage of grief, Sarah committed to finding real friends instead of "ideal" friends. She experimented with other people and groups, and practiced her new ability to distinguish love from its substitutes.

Paul the Apostle

We see a similar story with Paul, formerly known as Saul in the book of Acts, except Paul was the one persecuting the outsiders. Paul was in the religious right of his day, and was disgusted with a new sect of weirdos called Christians. He, being in the religious and social elite, took it upon himself to rid his society of a fast-growing group of people who looked, acted and believed differently. He was traveling from town to town rounding up Christians and throwing them into prison, when, out of the blue, he had a come-to-Jesus experience. "As he neared Damascus on his journey, suddenly a light from heaven flashed around him. He fell to the ground and heard a voice say to him, 'Saul, Saul, why do you persecute me?'" (Acts 9:3-4 NIV).

Once Paul saw the light, he could distinguish the real God from the imitation he was serving. He left everything that he knew: his status, position and the pressures to be perfect, and spent the next 14 years unlearning the ways of his past god-figures. He had something to say that was similar to what our friend Sarah said. Paul wrote, "Christ's love is greater than anyone can ever know, but I pray that you will be able to know that love. Then you can be filled with the fullness of God" (Ephesians 3:19 NCV). The love that Paul found in Christ transforms the outsider and the elitist alike into His beloved children. Jesus identifies Himself with the outsider, the one being persecuted by the religious elite "insiders."

God has a way of stripping us of deceptive religiosity, and goes to great lengths to love us. Sarah's world was turned upside down as she realized that God is not found in performance-based devotion. God appeared as a bright light and booming voice on the road to Damascas so that Paul could be saved from his religious fantasy of being the best religious person in the world.

Imitation religion is imitation relationship. There is nothing of substance and it leaves you hungrier, emptier and lonelier than you were before it came along. There may be zeal, but that is just like a mood altering drug that keeps you from feeling the loneliness of false intimacy.

How to Get Real

- Feel the pain. Usually we need something to happen to us like Sarah or Paul—something painful, before we break free of imitation. Something must knock us out of our alternate reality so we can see things clearly and accept God for who He really is, and not what we made Him to be. Feel the pain all the way through so you don't run to another fantasy to replace the old one.
- See the pain in the light of God's love. If the imitation is false intimacy, then what intimacies are available to you now that the old is gone? What part of Himself does God want to reveal to you? What part of your heart does He want to reveal to you?

- Use the pain to break through the old ways and into the reality of God's unconditional love, grace and freedom. Don't let the pain go to waste; let it energize you to make appropriate changes to your thoughts, attitudes and beliefs.

Questions for Self Reflection:

- Have you ever been tricked by imitation love? What were the results?
- Have you ever been an elite insider? What about a judged outsider?
- What do you think Jesus' perspective is on this subject?
- How do you know when you find God's love as opposed to imitation love?
- Have you ever lost something only to find that God has something better?
- What does it mean to be transformed? (See Romans 12:2; 2 Corinthians 3:18)

Intention Statement:

I am being transformed by the love of Christ as I depend on Him fully. I will prioritize the real over the ideal.

Extra Study:

Galatians 2:15–Galatians 3:6,
especially in *The Message* version

nineteen

Since You're Not Dead, Grow

"The kingdom of heaven is like a mustard seed, which a man took and sowed in his field, which indeed is the least of all the seeds; but when it is grown it is greater than the herbs and becomes a tree, so that the birds of the air come and nest in its branches."

Matthew 13:31-32 NKJV

One summer, I decided to plant sunflowers outside my kitchen window. I bought the seeds for the 6-foot sunflowers, planted them and then got busy and forgot them. Weeks went by before I went outside and rounded the corner to the isolated part of our yard where the seeds were planted. I was surprised to see four little sprouts poking their heads through dry cracked ground. They had not been watered since I planted them, and the ground was very hard, yet there they were—determined against all odds to grow! The dirt was so parched around them that it was actually broken and pushed up on all sides of the small green plants. I was amazed at the strength that the little plants had to push through the hard soil.

This made me think of the verse, "So neither he who plants nor he who waters is anything, but only God, who makes things grow" (1 Corinthians 3:7 NIV). Some of our deepest miseries come from lack of growth. Humans, from the time of conception, were created to flourish. But the god-figures in our lives may have stunted our growth, or were too caught up in their own lives to have any expectations for us. Thankfully, God doesn't forget about the seeds He has planted. God makes a way for us to grow, even when we think the conditions aren't quite right.

God knows how to organize our environment for growth. There are stubborn plants out there that refuse to grow. I remember a fig tree that Jesus cursed because of its refusal to grow and produce fruit properly—it shriveled up and died (Matthew 21:19). Then there are those plants that you just can't stop from growing.

People who are inclined toward growth do these things:

They see opportunity in every problem. We can easily focus on the problems and difficulties in life, thereby giving up the power to do anything about them. But if we see each problem as an opportunity for growth and expansion, we do ourselves a favor. Instead of letting our circumstances dictate to us how life will be, we tell our circumstances how life will be. It was as if my small sunflower plants said, "I will sprout. I will grow. I will not let this hard ground stop me."

They accept themselves. Brennan Manning writes, "The more fully we accept ourselves, the more successfully we begin to grow." He goes on to say, "When we accept ourselves for what we are, we decrease our hunger for power or the

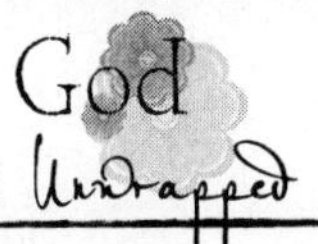

acceptance of others because our self-intimacy reinforces our inner sense of security. We are not preoccupied with being powerful or popular. We no longer fear criticism because we accept the reality of our human limitations. Once integrated, we are less often plagued with the desire to please others because simply being true to ourselves brings lasting peace. We are grateful for life and we deeply appreciate and love ourselves."[15] We can decide to accept ourselves, no matter what. This is unconditional love. If God loves and accepts us in this way, why don't we?

They ask for the truth, even if it hurts. There is a reason why most people are resistant to growth groups, counseling and performance evaluations—we don't want to hear anything negative about ourselves. But when we are open to the truth about ourselves, we have an immediate sense of power. There is nothing worse than trying to improve something, without knowing for sure what is not working. When we seek Jesus and live according to His ways, He will turn our lives right-side-up. Jesus says, "If you hold to my teaching, you are really my disciples. Then you will know the truth, and the truth will set you free" (John 8:31-32 NIV). Knowing the truth about ourselves will not devastate us, it will set us free.

They get around other healthy people. As we make ourselves available to other people and they invest their lives in us, we grow together. We begin to trust, loosen up, and start to let down our guard. When we do this in the context of relationships with other growers, we are fulfilling the proverb, "As iron sharpens iron, so a friend sharpens a

15 Manning, Brennan. *Ragamuffin Gospel*. Sisters, Oregon: Multnoma Publishers, 2000, P. 49,50.

friend" (Proverbs 27:17 NLT). There are areas of our life that will *only* grow in the context of relationship with others. There are parts of ourselves that will stay stuck and unfruitful if we do not accept the love of other people.

They take risks. Jesus referenced faith as a little mustard seed. And really, faith is the first step in this process of growth. To have faith the size of a mustard seed is to believe that God is who He says He is, and that you are who He says you are. Every bird must trust his wings and leave the nest if he wants to fly. If you take the first step of faith, then God makes the growing happen. Jesus said, "The kingdom of heaven is like a mustard seed, which a man took and sowed in his field, which indeed is the least of all the seeds; but when it is grown it is greater than the herbs and becomes a tree, so that the birds of the air come and nest in its branches" Matthew 13:31-32 NKJV).

"But what if you don't, because sometimes you won't?" (stealing a phrase from Doctor Seuss). What would possibly keep you from growing? Many of us know people who have been in church their entire adult life, but never grow to look like Jesus. Some ingredients of growth come easier to us than other ingredients. Usually, people will leave out the step that they fear the most, or that involves the most risk.

Common Fears that Keep Us from Growing

- Those who fear being controlled may rebel against God's ways. They will try at all odds to do it their way.
- Those who fear being abandoned may resist investing in healthy relationships. There are places in our heart that

will not grow unless they are grown in relationship with others.

- Those who have used guilt and obligation as their guide may be afraid to explore the desires of their heart. They have equated the desires of the heart to worldliness and self-centeredness.

- Those who fear being seen as weak may resist growth because growth requires them to admit shortcomings.

Taking small risks in the forward movement of growth produces all the fruit of the Spirit, but staying stuck in areas of immaturity produces lifeless limbs and bitter fruit. Trusting God is an expression of faith, and faith is what makes people grow. The more we trust God, the more we grow.

I once sat in on a therapy group of women at a transition home for battered women. Each of them had come out of destructive and violent relationships and was trying to get her feet on the ground again. The topic discussed that night was how to effectively manage conflict. The counselor asked for volunteers to role-play a conflict using a particular method of reflective listening and problem solving. The conflict had to do with some basic rules of the house—something very simple. Out of nine women, three volunteered to practice in front of the group. Each volunteer role-played and received feedback, and later commented on her experience of the exercise. They each said that just the thought of conflict brought on feelings of intense fear. But each volunteer pushed through her fears in order to reap the reward of growth. Afterward, they all remarked how much stronger and more confident they felt.

This teaches us to take a risk, and push through the hard stuff to reap the reward.

Questions for Self Reflection:

- In what three areas have you seen God grow you up in the last year?
- What problem are you facing in which you would like to find the opportunity?
- In what ways will you get around healthy people?
- What risk will you take in response to reading this?

Intention Statement:

Today, I purpose to grow in every situation:
to achieve and excel, and learn from my mistakes.

Extra Study:

Romans 12:2; 2 Corinthians 3:18; 2 Corinthians 4:16-18

twenty
Don't Be Afraid of Your Freedom

"He is so rich in kindness and grace that he purchased our freedom with the blood of his Son and forgave our sins."

Ephesians 1:7 NLT

All over the world, in places like Southeast Asia, Eastern Europe, India and even within the borders of the US, there are slaves, sold and purchased and either coerced or forced to do things against their will. Commonly, young women fall prey to the deception of a slave trafficker who promises decent work and good opportunity in the city. Instead, the traffickers bring young women and men alike to brothels far from their homes where they are sold like cattle. The women are forced to be prostitutes with little provision and no freedom. Organizations like International Justice Mission and Pure Hope work with local authorities to rescue slaves of all ages, restore them to their families, and prosecute the criminals involved.

Spiritually speaking, this happens to every person, regardless of position, status or place. The Bible states that,

"God sent him [Jesus] to buy freedom for us who were slaves to the law, so that he could adopt us as his very own children" (Galatians 4:5-7 NLT). We have been deceived and have been slaves to sin and to the law, having no power to release ourselves from the burden of guilt. But God rescued us through Christ's death and resurrection, and restores us to our spiritual home in Him.

But sometimes we lose sight of those spiritual freedoms. We get wrapped up in the expectations of other people, the duties and obligations of our roles, and disappointment in ourselves and other people. We live more like a slave, chained by fear, and we doubt that we can be as free as God wants to make us.

Living in freedom is living from the "want to" instead of the "have to." A man said about his wife one day in my office, "I have to come home every night by 6:00 or else she'll be mad at me." Then the wife responded, "Well, I have to invite his parents for every holiday or else he'll be mad at me." Each made their spouse the master, relegating themselves to the position of slave.

Slave language is: "I have to work long hours or else my boss will think I'm a loaf."

"I have to serve on the PTA because there's no one else to do it."

Free Language is: "I want to come home from work so I can spend time with my family." "I want to have a good work ethic, so I put in extra time." "I want to influence the school for good, so I'll volunteer."

"Wants" always come from desire and love. "Have-tos" come out of obligation. Obligations drain energy and passion and cause resentment. "Wants" create more energy, ideas, opportunity, and love.

This self-assessment will help you identify where you are in your pursuit of spiritual freedom. Where you are at now is not where you used to be, and is not where you will be in the future. But getting a good snapshot of where you are today can help you identify the blind spots, the potholes, and also where you want to be. This assessment specifically addresses your spiritual freedom in the areas of judgments, thoughts, relationships, family, compulsive behaviors, and your relationship with God. It is intended to provide increased self-awareness, which is an important step in personal and spiritual growth. You'll discover areas that keep you from experiencing the spiritual freedom that God wants you to have.

Please select the option that is true most of the time. Choosing quickly and spontaneously will provide a more accurate description than belabored answers.

Judgments

1. Are you able to make thorough decisions in a reasonable amount of time?

   Usually Sometimes Seldom

2. Are you able to make decisions without asking others for their opinion?

   Usually Sometimes Seldom

3. Are you able to hear and follow your intuition in a way that helps and protects you?

   Usually Sometimes Seldom

4. Are you able to listen to "red flag" moments even if it means being impolite?

   Usually Sometimes Seldom

Thoughts

5. Are you able to interact with peers without analyzing and worrying at a later point about what was said?

   Usually Sometimes Seldom

6. Do you regularly tell yourself encouraging things that motivate and inspire?

   Usually Sometimes Seldom

7. Do you regularly accept yourself as being human in the face of mistakes and short comings?

   Usually Sometimes Seldom

Relationships

8. Are you able to say "no" in your closest relationships without experiencing guilt?

   Usually Sometimes Seldom

9. Are you able to say no in other relationships, such as extended family, church friends, or acquaintances without guilt?

   Usually Sometimes Seldom

10. Are you able to be honest about your feelings of discomfort, reservations, or limitations with the people around you?

    Usually Sometimes Seldom

11. Are you able to accept someone's "no" without feeling personally rejected?

    Usually Sometimes Seldom

12. Are you able to connect with others in a meaningful way without the compulsion to please them, control them or change them?

    Usually Sometimes Seldom

Childhood Family

13. When you are with your family of origin, are you able to respond to them as an adult, as opposed to feeling like a child?

    Usually Sometimes Seldom

14. Are you able to live your adult life without fear of becoming like the members of your childhood family ?

Usually Sometimes Seldom

15. Are you able to appreciate the good parts of your family of origin and forgive the painful parts?

    Usually Sometimes Seldom

Compulsive Behaviors

16. How often do you resist temptation to self-soothe in unhealthy ways (drinking, shopping, gaming, illicit images, food, etc)?

    Usually Sometimes Seldom

17. Are you able to meet your core needs for belonging, esteem, and self-actualization in healthy ways (i.e. relationships, using talents, volunteering, etc)?

    Usually Sometimes Seldom

18. Are you able to admit compulsions, forgive yourself and enlist someone's help in overcoming them?

    Usually Sometimes Seldom

Relationship with God

19. How often do you give yourself permission to need God and ask for help?

Usually Sometimes Seldom

20. Are you able to talk to God anytime, even when you have fallen short or sinned?

    Usually Sometimes Seldom

21. Are you able to forgive yourself, or let yourself off the hook when you fall short, without harboring self blame and regret?

    Usually Sometimes Seldom

22. Do you feel a passion and desire when using your God-given talents?

    Usually Sometimes Seldom

23. Do you feel a sense of connectedness and desire in your quiet time, as opposed to obligation, rigidity or academic Bible study?

    Usually Sometimes Seldom

24. Are you able to ask forgiveness and forgive others regarding hurtful situations without bitterness, unresolved anger, or passive aggressiveness?

    Usually Sometimes Seldom

25. How often are you at peace from worry regarding your core needs of provision and protection, trusting God in all things?

Usually Sometimes Seldom

Scoring Yourself

Review your answers giving yourself 3 points for Usually, 2 points for Sometimes, and 1 point for Seldom.

Your Score ______________

75-60 You feel a sense of spiritual freedom in many areas of your life. You are able to make strong decisions and accept yourself when you make weak decisions. You feel differentiated from those around you in a way that allows you to say no without guilt and to say yes with love. You are able to be at peace with yourself, not setting super-human expectations. You are usually able to connect with people you care about without losing yourself. You have experienced a sense of healing from past hurts, and are able to forgive people, allowing you to live fully in the present. You usually are able to self-soothe in healthy ways, and are able to enlist others for support when needed. You feel a sense of spiritual freedom with God, allowing yourself to experience God in new and fresh ways. You do not feel a sense of rigidity, restriction, or rejection based on performance, but instead, a mutual exchange of love, energy, and purpose with the Father.

59-40 You know what spiritual freedom feels like in some areas of your life; however, you would like much more. You have some difficulty making decisions, either waiting a long time or acting impulsively. You are sometimes able to say no to others, but still don't feel the freedom you want to in regard to other people. Sometimes you feel compelled to please others, even if it puts you in an awkward position. You sometimes really like the person you are and take pride in accomplishments, however you still struggle with self-blame and doubt. You are aware that your childhood family affects your present life, but you want to work through the past so it has less of a negative effect. When you have painful feelings, you sometimes treat them with unhealthy habits that make you feel worse in the long run. Your relationship with God is evident and helpful to you; however, you have questions and doubts about God and your role as a Christian. You may view being a Christian as an obligation rather than a desire.

<u>39-25</u> You rarely experience a sense of spiritual freedom in your life, and feel beat down a lot of the time. You have a lot of difficulty making decisions, being fearful of making the wrong one. You have trouble saying "no" to others, sometimes getting yourself into awkward, even dangerous situations. You don't feel good about yourself, and you have negative self-talk. You want to connect with other people, but aren't sure how to make healthy boundaries in a relationship. You have a lot of hurts from the past that keep you stuck in a pattern of repetition. When you are lonely or hurting, you turn to things and people that are not healthy for you, often making things worse. Your relationship with God is not all you expected it would be, and you may even feel like you have disappointed God or vice versa.

Questions for Self Reflection:

- In what areas do you want more spiritual freedom?
- In what areas do you feel like a slave (to other's expectations, to past pain, to unhealthy dependencies, to perfectionism, etc.)?
- How have you grown in the past year in the area of spiritual freedom?

Intention Statement:

My spiritual freedom has been purchased at a great price, and I am determined to live in it and strive to give it to others.

Extra Study:

Colossians 2:13-23; Psalm 119:45; Romans 8:21

twenty-one

Stopping the Stopper

"Then he showed me Joshua the high priest standing before the angel of the LORD, and Satan standing at his right side to accuse him."

Zechariah 3:1 NIV

Novelist G.K. Chesterton said, "Fairy Tales are more than true; not because they tell us that dragons exist, but because they tell us that dragons can be beaten." In other words, children know that there are monsters, dragons and ghosts. Have you ever tried to calm a child's bedtime fears saying, "There's no such thing as monsters"? This method usually does little to calm a child, maybe because God has imprinted His story on our soul. From a very young age, we know about good, about evil, and about power. The question on our lips is, "Who wins?"

I remember when my own children struggled with bedtime fears. The only way that they truly overcame their fears was when I entered their world, saw the monster as they saw it, and helped them defeat it. My children and I prowled around their bedroom floor and practiced our growls. We imagined the scary monster as a big monster balloon, and with a prick of a pin, the monster deflated and disappeared. I knew that I couldn't convince them out of their fear, so I worked to empower them in the midst of their fear, and with time, they rested easily.

There is a real dragon, though: one that the Bible talks about as a murderer, a liar and a lion that roams about seeking whom he may devour; basically stopping Christians from doing God's work. It's the devil. The characterization of Satan is somewhat laughable in our world today, with pitchfork in hand and wagging tail behind. To the popular culture that has cut its theological teeth on the Saturday Night Live skit of the Church Lady, Satan is a distant mythical character found in rock music played backwards, sitting on people's shoulders, and on Marilyn Manson's stage. But the Bible teaches differently. The Bible says, "Put on the full armor of God so that you can take your stand against the devil's schemes. For our struggle is not against flesh and blood, but against the rulers, against the authorities, against the powers of this dark world and against the spiritual forces of evil in the heavenly realms" (Ephesians 6:11-12 NIV).

One way that Satan stops Christians is by accusing them of past sins. Joshua, a man found in the Old Testament book of Zechariah, was chosen as the nation's high priest. Zechariah was a prophet and teacher, and had a vision about Joshua, not unlike the dreams many people have today. A teacher friend of mine told me that every summer before school starts, she has dreams of herself standing naked in front of the classroom. Feeling exposed and embarrassed in the dream, she tries to cover herself up with class notes. Then she wakes up. Have you ever dreamed something like that?

Zechariah's vision gets to the heart of Joshua's insecurities, just like our dreams do.

In the center of the Zechariah's vision are three main characters: the Lord, who is surrounded by select commanding angels, Joshua who represents humanity, and Satan, the Accuser. When Joshua comes on the scene, he is wearing filthy clothes, but not just your ordinary spaghetti sauce-stain-kind-of-filth. The stuff on Joshua was the kind of filth you find on your carpet after your dog ate bad fish. So Joshua was pretty repugnant.

Zechariah records, "*The Accuser, Satan, was there at the angel's right hand, making accusations against Joshua*" (Zechariah 3:1 NLT). I imagine Satan's script during the vision to be similar to what we hear in our own heads like: "Do you think God is really going to use you? What are you supposed to be, a high priest or something? You look more like something from Judas Priest. Look at you, you're disgusting!" Then speaking to the Lord, I imagine Satan's rhetoric to be, "I have a list of the sins that this man unashamedly reveled in! Smell him! He's weak! He's nothing! He's a waste!"

Accusatory language feeds our guilt. We know we are soiled, we know we have fallen short, and we know that we are helpless to change the past. The satanic message sops wet with reminders of the acts that produced the shame in the first place, and leaves us with a feeling of hopelessness.

We might be ok if we were only accused of everyday sins that everyone seems to commit. But the accusations that are most wearisome are the ones that point to the sins we really regret. Like a pack of hounds sniffing out the runaway convict, the accusations find us, judge us, and imprison us once again. The Bible describes Satan as the accuser of Christian brothers and sisters, and he does so before God both day and night (Revelation 12:10 NKJV). Even after confession and repentance, the guilt of our sin can haunt even our happiest moments because we have an unremitting accuser.

In this vision, Joshua presents himself to the Lord just as he is, with all of his sordid, Babylonian pagan history and the residue that it left behind. The Lord, without discussion, quickly and decidedly rebukes the Accuser, by saying, "*I, the LORD, reject your accusations, Satan. Yes, the LORD, who has chosen Jerusalem, rebukes you*" (Zechariah 3:2 NLT). Joshua was not required to give his defense and no character witnesses were asked to stand up for him. Nothing was required from Joshua at all, except to appear. His Advocate and his Judge, the Lord, spoke strongly in his favor and with a word, silenced the Accuser's sulfuric tongue.

The Lord then cleansed Joshua of his sin, clothed him with a clean robe, and spoke of his value. He charged him with obedience and gave him a promise of reward and blessing. He said, "*If you follow my ways and carefully serve me, then you will be given authority over my Temple and its courtyards*" (Zechariah 3:7 NLT). The Lord also made Joshua a symbol of the Christ to come, giving the people of that day a picture of the King that would one day save their people, and indeed, the world. Joshua, once stained unrecognizably with sin and brought low with accusations, was given the privilege of representing the coming Messiah. Pretty cool, right?

I love Joshua's story because I can relate to it. We all know what it feels like to be accused. We have all tried to

pray and have involuntarily seen the flashbacks of our sin on our mind's screen. But Joshua didn't clean up before he came to the Lord. The Lord did the cleaning and gave him new clothes too. Joshua's history didn't disqualify him from serving and ruling and fulfilling God's purpose for him as priest. God desires that we be free from the accusations of the enemy, to be free from the sin that muddied us, and to go forward with purpose.

If you are haunted by guilt and remorse, remember who it is that accuses you. Remember Who it is that has swift, decisive authority over the Accuser. When the accusations come, there is no need for a convincing argument or more confession. Regurgitating scripture is generally unhelpful if the heart hides in unbelief. Stand firm in your position of "forgiven."

Joshua was not alone in this vision. The scripture goes on to reference Joshua's friends who witnessed the scene before them. Take a look at what God said to Joshua, "Careful, High Priest Joshua—both you and your friends sitting here with you, for your friends are in on this, too! Here's what I'm doing next: I'm introducing my servant Branch. I'll strip this land of its filthy sin, all at once, in a single day. At that time, everyone will get along with one another, with friendly visits across the fence, friendly visits on one another's porches" (Zechariah 3:8-10 MSG).

God never intended for us to live in the isolated world of our own heads. This drama between the Accuser and Joshua was shared with Joshua's friends. By inviting our friends into our struggles and sins, habits and hang-ups, they can help us replace the old god-figures in our lives with acceptance and forgiveness. The forgiveness part is already done— Jesus takes care of that and we are forgiven whether we feel like we are or not. Simply said, if we are having trouble "feeling forgiven" then we probably have not allowed some trusted people in our lives to be our witnesses and confirm the process of forgiveness.

New God-figures

James writes in his letter, "Therefore, confess your sins to one another, and pray for one another so that you may be healed" (James 5:16 NASB). To *confess* means to disclose one's faults, or to unburden one's sins or the state of one's conscience.[16] Confessing our sins to a friend is one way to unload the burden of guilt and shame. Confession probably evokes some fear of judgment or rejection from others, but really it is the thing that sets freedom in motion. We "come clean" to someone else and get healed in the process. Zechariah's vision clearly communicates that God stands against Satan's accusations against us, and He uses godly people around us to complete the process. These godly friends become new god-figures to replace the old and help us assimilate the loving characteristics of God.

Accusations and doubt don't just make a person feel bad, they suck the drive out of a person. When you are making a difference, working toward justice and mercy, drawing healthy boundaries or stepping out in faith, you *will* experience accusatory thoughts of fear and doubt. Like

16 Merriam-Webster, Inc. *Merriam-Webster's Collegiate Dictionary.* Eleventh ed. Springfield, Mass. : Merriam-Webster, Inc., 2003.

Joshua, once God has motivated you to take your rightful place in His plan, the Accuser will come. If *you* are defeated, then your *movement* is defeated. Don't let that happen. Don't let the Stopper stop you.

Questions for Self Reflection:

- Have you ever felt accused and attacked?
- Have your thoughts ever been loaded with self-doubt or God-doubt?
- Write down familiar accusatory statements that have stopped you in the past.
- When you feel accused or condemned, what statements will help to combat that feeling? (I am forgiven. God does not accuse me. I don't listen to liars.)

Intention Statement:

I know who I am. I am more than a conqueror. I am an overcomer. I am who Christ says I am. I will invite others into my life to remind me.

Extra Study:

Galatians 2:20; Philippians 3:9;
2 Corinthians 11:14-15; 1 Peter 2:9

twenty-two

What a Cute Little Idol, Does It Have a Name?

"So long as man remains free he strives for nothing so incessantly and so painfully as to find someone to worship."

Dostoyevsky, *Brother's Karasmov*

For a few years, my husband and I had the opportunity to live in Germany. We traveled Europe on the cheap and came back to the states with a depleted savings account and a full photo album worth every penny.

One of our trips took us to Pompeii near the Bay of Naples, Italy. Anyone who has ever visited will agree that Pompeii is a provocative and illustrative look into the 1st century AD of Roman culture. Incredibly preserved and expansive, this ruined city is complete with mansions, a coliseum, a market place, shops, public baths, brothels, a theatre and an exercise arena. It also is home to Mount Vesuvius, a volcano which

erupted in 79 AD and killed up to 20,000 residents of the Mediterranean town, sealing the city in ash for hundreds of years before excavation started in the 1700's. Seeing the preserved shapes of bodies in their last throws of life is more than a little haunting.

The homes owned by the economically elite were adorned with frescos, gardens, and extravagantly tiled fountains serving as shrines for the family's personal idol. Smaller shrines for idols lined the streets and decked the doorways. A vast open air forum spattered with columns was home to elaborate temples for Apollo, Jupiter, Vespasian, the Lares, and Isis. Most were fitted with altars for animal sacrifice. The Pompeian people were very religious.

One ancient god that was difficult to ignore, was Priapus, the god of sex and fertility. Erotic frescoes adorned walls of homes and brothels alike, depicting him in various forms. My husband and I stifled giggles and jokes at—well, the sheer size of the object of worship. Pompeii was kind of a sexual smorgasbord. A part of the people's devotion to Priapus was the indulgence in every sexual appetite. Brothels, as commonplace as vegetable markets, were serviced by prostitutes, most of whom were indentured servants, similar to our modern day sex slave. Under the window of an ancient brothel, an inscription depicted the going rate for sex with a prostitute—the equivalent of the price of bread.

The folks in Pompeii did the same thing we do today, just in a culturally different way. We look for the thing that will fill us up, and then we worship it. I heard a man speak of his wife, "She fills my bucket!" I heard the wife say, "But his

bucket is a bottomless pit!" The pursuit of this "filling up" is otherwise known as "worship".

The word *worship* means "to regard with great or extravagant respect, honor, or devotion."[17] An idol is the object of that worship. On the shirt-tail of a natural and God-given need—the need for security and love—comes the detestable devotion to the created object. It happens so automatically and seamlessly that we are hardly aware that we have placed our dependence on the created thing instead of the Creator *of* the thing. It's like worshipping bread instead of the baker.

Back to Pompeii

The weary traveler to ancient Pompeii saw the source of his provision in the brothel and paid homage to the created, carved and painted god of Priapus by satisfying his sexual appetites. The people of Pompeii celebrated sexuality to the point of seeking life within its practices. The traveler sought the thrill, the escape, the chance to feel like a desirable man. Feeling this way was his bread of life—until the bread ran out and he needed more. And then upon receiving the bread again, he would most assuredly find that it tasted a bit stale. He would convince himself that his need for bread was a good and holy need, but somehow satisfaction was just out of reach. He just knew that if he kept it up, he would be satisfied somehow. He then would discover that the bread could be served with meat, and, if he had enough money, he could have cheese and wine with it too. Alas, soon he would find, to his disappointment and fury, that the meat he was served

17 Merriam-Webster, Inc. *Merriam-Webster's Collegiate Dictionary*. Eleventh ed. Springfield, Mass. : Merriam-Webster, Inc., 2003.

spoiled and his wine turned to vinegar. He would then promptly leave that brothel, and would quite possibly leave Pompeii all together, having heard on the street that the girls in Ephesus were much more friendly.

What a Cute Little Idol, Does It Have a Name?

Idolatry didn't suffocate in ash with the people of Pompeii. It may not be in the form of statues today, but its allure is just as palpable. Romantic love, power, status, money, possessions, esteem, adoration, and substances can all turn into idols—anything that we look to instead of God.

I get caught up in it, just like you. For me, I like the Stuff goddess—big, brand-y, beautiful Stuff. Shape-shifting, never-ending, not-enough, lusty-Stuff. She's gorgeous, you should see her. I built her a temple so I could proudly display her and her entourage within its walls. She requires very little sacrifice, really—just habitual over-spending and a deep devotion to designer jeans and bags. Paying homage to her is such a high… until the bill comes in the mail and then I hate her, and all her little friends too!

What's *Your* Idol's Name?

These little objects of our affection never give back what they take. They are so unworthy of our worship. The Bible says that people who worship idols will, "prostitute themselves to their gods and sacrifice to them" (Exodus 34:15-16 NIV), giving to their idols the most sacred parts of themselves. When we grasp for things, people, and power over God, we not only give them our devotion, we give them our souls. Jesus says,

"And what do you benefit if you gain the whole world but lose your own soul? Is anything worth more than your soul?" (Matthew 16:26 NLT). The word *soul* means the immaterial essence or a person's total self.[18] Jesus isn't just talking about losing eternal salvation or eternal life, in essence, Jesus is asking, "What kind of deal is it to get everything you want but lose yourself?" (Matthew 16:26 MSG).

The Bible warns, "...do not make for yourselves an idol in the form of anything the LORD your God has forbidden. For the LORD your God is a consuming fire, a jealous God" (Deuteronomy 4:23-24 NIV). He is the only one worthy of our worship, and the only one that will satisfy. God doesn't share our heart with idols. All worship and devotion are due Jesus who loved us and gave us life.

From Idolatry to Relationship

So, how do we shift from worshipping the created thing to worshipping the Creator? Well, for me, clinging more tightly to God is a first step. Reading about Jesus' character and shockingly successful ministry makes my stuff so insignificant in comparison to His ageless influence and power. Giving away what I'm tempted to hoard is a freedom like no other. Allowing God's work to be fulfilled in me as I trust Him with my insecurities and fears shows me that my idol was not only keeping me from God, but also from myself. Soon, as the obstacle between God and me is removed, my passions and purpose return with fervor, and the good life is restored.

---

18 Merriam-Webster, Inc. *Merriam-Webster's Collegiate Dictionary*. Eleventh ed. Springfield, Mass. : Merriam-Webster, Inc., 2003.

Questions for Self Reflection:

- In what way have you tried to fill the hole in your soul with worldly pleasures? How do you feel after the pleasure is gone?
- Would you like to invite God to fill that hole instead of the alternative?
- Are you addicted to someone or something? Is someone or something your "bread" of life?
- How much time, money, and devotion does that someone or something take to maintain? How much of yourself must you give away to maintain it?

Intention Statement:

I will worship God alone, depending on His life-provision every day of my life, seeking no other to thrill me, satisfy me or give me purpose.

Extra Study:

Isaiah 41:28-29; Isaiah 42:6-9;
Romans 1:23; 1 Thessalonians 1:9

twenty-three

Meritage God

"They worshiped cosmic forces—sky gods and goddesses—and frequented the sex-and-religion shrines of Baal. They even sank so low as to offer their own sons and daughters as sacrificial burnt offerings! They indulged in all the black arts of magic and sorcery. In short, they prostituted themselves to every kind of evil available to them. And God had had enough."

2 Kings 17:16-17 MSG

"Roxanne...you don't have to put out the red light..."

The Police

My husband and I were on a weekend getaway without the kids, and states away from home. I had never visited California's countryside before, so you can imagine my delight as the fog of San Francisco cleared and romantic Napa Valley appeared before me. The vineyards blanketed before us like a patchwork quilt of greens and browns, and were a gorgeous example of human ingenuity intertwining with divine

design. During a tasting stop, a friendly gentleman, eager to talk about his wines, explained the concept of meritage. Have you heard of it?

Red Meritage wine must be made from a blend of Cabernet Sauvignon, Cabernet Franc, Merlot, Malbec and Petit Verdot, the classic Bordeaux grape varieties. The proportions may vary, but at least three of the grape varieties must be used to call it a meritage. Basically, Meritage is a blend. The vintner said, in a poeticism that fit the spirit of the trip, "In a good meritage wine, one grape should not overpower the other—it should be a perfect balance of the different grapes represented. You should be able to explore the hidden secrets of each grape within the perfect blending of all of them."[19] His quote was so good, I wrote it down.

The young man may have had a secret knowledge of how relationships work best, too. Indeed, the marital relationship thrives as both people are equally represented, neither overpowers the other, and hidden secrets are discovered in the safety of their unity with God as the blending force that makes it all work. This is how relationships work best.

In the book of Hosea, however, we are given a different example of a marital relationship—one that we should not emulate. It starts with God's command to the prophet Hosea to marry a prostitute as a symbol of the people's spiritual adultery against God. Talk about arranged marriages. Anyway, God chose the context of marital love to describe His devotion to His people. Sometimes it's easier to see God

---

19 I wrote his quote down the moment I heard it and kept it in my purse. That is why I remember it, if you know what I mean.

in a Father role, but here, God is clear about His role as Husband. In essence, our worship of God is more like a long term marriage relationship than it is an act or duty of service.

As Hosea's story unfolds, his bride does not return love to him, but gives it away to others and breaks their sacred bond. Hosea records the unfaithful wife as saying, "I will go after my lovers, who give me my bread and my water, My wool and my linen, My oil and my drink" (Hosea 2:5 NKJV). God commiserated with Hosea when He talks to him about the Israelites, saying, "'She decked herself with her earrings and jewelry, and went after her lovers; But Me she forgot,' says the LORD" (Hosea 2:13 NKJV).

Gomer, Hosea's wife, thought and acted like a prostitute, and was married in contract only. A prostitute is familiar with being used, violated and taken for granted. Maybe you can relate. Maybe the god-figures in your life used, mistreated and took advantage of you, and it's hard to stop thinking and acting like a prostitute—being married to God in contract only. The pay off for Gomer was that she never had to be vulnerable with Hosea.

As you know by now, God wants more than a contract, He wants your heart. We each have a deep soulful desire to be connected to the Divine. This soul desire is a beautiful ache to come back home to the place we belong. The Bible says, "Look to the rock from which you were hewn, and to the hole of the pit from which you were dug. Look to Abraham your father, And to Sarah who bore you" (Isaiah 51:1-2 NKJV). We are cut from divinity and presented as a pure and spotless bride, destined for a love relationship with Him.

There are times when trusting God feels very uncomfortable, even painful, because we are making ourselves vulnerable to Him and His love and the times we have been vulnerable with other god-figures, we've been hurt. But God is the faithful groom. He doesn't use us for His gain or gratification. Jesus says, "Anyone who drinks the water I give will never thirst—not ever. The water I give will be an artesian spring within, gushing fountains of endless life" (John 4:13-14 MSG). If we only knew that we already have all that we ever need.

Jesus says, "He who believes in Me, as the Scripture has said, out of his heart will flow rivers of living water" (John 7:38 NKJV). Once we really come home and begin to live in this place of freedom and life, in the full knowledge that every need we have is completely satisfied by God, then we start acting like it, too. We don't look to other people to value us, so we can feel valued. We value ourselves enough, and we stop attracting people who don't value us. We don't look to others to make us feel important. We already know we are important and we will stop acting like we don't really matter.

As a bride of Christ, we invite the public praise and admiration that is due us singing, "She is clothed with strength and dignity, and she laughs without fear of the future" (Proverbs 31:25 NLT).

God desires a relationship with us. Couched within that relationship is dignity and value, safety and adventure, life and happiness. Within the meritage of that relationship, we are free to be who we really are, not selling out to what other people want us to be, and not dominated or controlled. "For

in Him we live and move and have our being" (Acts 17:28 NKJV), He does not overpower us; instead, He brings out the best in us. He respects and honors what we bring to the relationship and He blends himself into everything we do, giving the relationship a flavor of divinity and hope to all who experience it. He says to the wayward wife, "you will call me 'my husband' instead of 'my master'" (Hosea 2:16 NLT). God calls His people to experience something radically different than anything the world can give.

Questions for Self Reflection:

- How have you trusted other things or people in the hopes of getting love from them?
- What part of yourself have you lost in order to make a deal with this idol?
- What is it hard to trust God with? Your marriage, job, kids, future? Your heart?
- How is it easier to seek after other things instead of trusting God with your heart? What things do you seek after?

Intention Statement:

I am valuable and will act as if I know my own value.
I will choose to draw close to God and trust Him,
because He is faithful.

Extra Study:

Isaiah 50:10; Isaiah 64:4; Hosea 12:6; John 14:1;
Romans 4:5; Romans 9:32; Romans 15:13

twenty-four
The Space

"Between stimulus and response there is a space. In that space is our power to choose our response. In our response lies our growth and our freedom."

Viktor Frankl

Joe's Story

Joe came to coaching sessions, wanting to work on his job stress. I said, "Yeah, you and me both, buddy! You should see the people I work with!" No, I didn't really say that out loud, I just thought it. Anyway, he was in management and was considered successful and respected in his corporate circle. In less than two months time, though, he had been socked with a breach of contract lawsuit, an employee grievance of age discrimination, and a client complaint for being unprofessional. He was willing to own up to his mistakes and knew how he could have avoided the recent events. "But," he explained, "so much is expected of me and the work load is so heavy since the new contract, that I have to work fast to get things done."

I asked, "And it is when you work so fast to get things done that you make mistakes that you normally would have avoided?"

"Yes," he said, "and the people around me aren't doing their job, so I have to do it for them!"

Ahhh, that was the rub. My bright, capable client was getting sucked into the control trap. He felt the pressures of the additional workload, started to sense his world spinning with unrealistic expectations, and began the natural process of controlling things so he wouldn't feel so out of control. He numbed his fears with "doing things" (watch-dogging e-mails, making quick decisions, handling other people's messes, all the while isolating himself from his wife). Normally, he was great at his job, but in the face of added pressures, he felt the need to do "their" job too. This is when mistakes were made, alliances damaged, and resentments harbored.

I have experienced similar controlling urges. For example, when I worry about my kids', husband's, or friends' personal choices, I am tempted to control through "advising" or "lecturing". This comes quite naturally, mind you, and I am very good at it. But the reason I do it is out of fear, not love. I feel afraid that something bad will happen if I don't "step in," and I feel the over-responsibility and pressure to convince them of my view point. These are controlling behaviors that sabotage relationships, and stress me out too.

Instead, if I sit with the discomfort and insecurity, I am forced to deal with my fears head-on. At that point, the anxiety I feel is compounded by withdrawal-type feelings. Getting worse before it gets better, fear wants to convince me that I should start controlling things again or else bad things will happen and I'll ultimately be a bad wife, mother, and friend. Facing the possibility of these 'bad things' forces me to depend on God again. God always provides me with space to grapple with these things and uncover the truth about them. The question I often ask myself in the middle of these times is, "What is the worst thing that could happen? Would God still be God? Will God still value me?" The answer is always "yes".

In the space between stimulus and response, Joe also learned how to sit with powerlessness. He learned to practice self control and trust God with the rest. He got right to work on his issues, because he really wanted to feel better and work better. He found ways to keep himself calmer at work (empowering), and to say "no" to things that weren't his to do (very empowering). He resisted checking e-mails past 8 pm and talked through work issues with his wife. After making some progress, he was offered a promotion, and he was ready to take it.

God-figures

Joe was raised by a single mother and had to grow up early to take care of himself. His mother often worked long shifts, and his father rarely visited or helped with child support. Joe became disillusioned with his father by his teen years and was determined never to be like him. As an adult, Joe was terrified of being seen as a poor or lazy worker. Because he learned at an early age to be self-sufficient, he believed that it was all up to him, and he couldn't rely on anyone else to do their part. He learned not to trust others, but to only trust himself.

There are many reasons why we are controlling instead of self-controlled—our god-figures being just one of them. Whatever the cause, let's look at an example of how Jesus surrendered control so we have a picture of how to do it ourselves.

The KING OF THE UNIVERSE... in a teeny weeny body

Jesus, God of the universe, gave up His rights, privileges and abundance as King of Heaven to be a dependent and finite child. Diane Langburg said, "Limitation is required for expansion. The Infinite gathered Himself up in a womb. All Glory lay Himself in a barn. All Power became a toddler. All Love was slain before time began its march." She continues, "He who never grows weary knew tiredness. He who was infinite and eternal submitted to the clock. He who was perfect and sinless bore our sins. Our God limited himself on all of these fronts and more and the resulting expansion is mindboggling."[20]

Jesus says, "For whoever desires to save his life will lose it, but whoever loses his life for My sake will find it" (Matthew 16:25 NKJV). Jesus knew what giving up His own life really meant and the sacrifice that came with it. He is trustworthy to handle our fears of doing the same. When we give up trying to control the uncontrollable, we invite God into our limitations. This invitation gives us the freedom from

20 Diane Lindburg, PhD was a plenary speaker at the American Association of Christian Counselors World Conference in 2005. These words were taken from Counsel CD produced by AACC.

pressure and over-responsibility, and gives Jesus access to expand our limitations. Limitation is required for expansion. In my estimation, self-control is a difficult enough task by itself, why seek to control everything else?

Controlling God: An Ancient Pasttime

Sometimes at the altar of spiritual sacrifice, we are tempted to use our worship as a means to control God. We follow as many rules as we have figured out so as to receive optimal blessing from God. We read the books, we do the Bible study, we serve in church, teach our kids Bible verses, and we give to the poor. We serve others before ourselves, meet needs, die to self, walk the extra mile, turn the other cheek, and give our bodies as living sacrifices. We do a lot of good things.

We put a lot of stock into these good things. Martin Luther, the reformist of the 1500s who changed the way Christians understood their faith, wrote, "If we doubt or do not believe that God is gracious to us and is pleased with us, or if we presumptuously expect to please Him only through and after our works, then it is all pure deception, outwardly honoring God, but inwardly setting up self as a false [savior]..."[21]

The myth is, "If I am a good Christian and do the things that good Christians do, then I will make God pleased with me, thereby avoiding tragedy and receiving blessing." In essence, this person attempts to control her unmanageable world and her "unpredictable" God with her good behavior. She, by working and volunteering and being as good as she can, believes that it is her good works that keep her afloat.

21 Luther, Martin. *A Treatise on Good Works*, 1520.

Thankfully, God in His grace toward us, gently leads us through experiences that teach us that it is not our good works that make us safe in this life and the next. In fact, His idea of "safe" is different than ours. Margaret Alter writes,

> God is interested in our ultimate freedom, abundant life imbedded in finitude. The gospel allows us no righteous certainty controlled by our own manipulations. Jesus consistently disrupts certainty with its suspicions and guarantees. He interrupts its self-perpetuating cycle of anxiety and judgment.
>
> He invites us to live by trusting in God and surrendering the illusion of control. His gospel speaks directly to two primary human fears: fear of abandonment and fear of finitude. Wooed by God's longing for relationship with us, we are assured of the presence of the Spirit. Entering into our finitude in all its poverty and suffering, we are invited to see life in the light of the resurrection. Our lives and deaths are in God's hands.[22]

The questions is, "Are God's hands good?"

Remember the Serenity Prayer? I was trying to recall it one day while calming myself for a needle prick. A lab technician prepared me with information about the radioactive material she was about to inject into my veins that would disqualify me from hugging my children for about 12 hours, and I was

---

22 Alter, Margaret, G. *Resurrection Psychology: An understanding of human personality based on the life and teachings of Jesus*. Chicago, IL: Loyola University Press, 1994. P. 102-103.

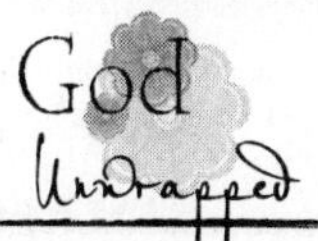

feeling a bit anxious. I closed my eyes, and said out loud, "I wish I could remember the Serenity Prayer right now."

The lab technician apparently had needed it before, and without hesitation repeated, "God grant me the serenity to accept the things I cannot change; courage to change the things I can; and wisdom to know the difference." I caught her eyes, sighed, and readied myself for not only the prick, but the diagnosis that might come with it. I had to ask myself, even if the worst happens, do I believe God to be good?

As Christians, our idea of "good" is challenged by real life events—early death, sickness, divorce, foreclosure, and natural disasters. These things happen to Christians and non-Christians alike. Sometimes "bad" things cannot be avoided. The Bible says, "those who hope in the LORD will renew their strength. They will soar on wings like eagles; they will run and not grow weary, they will walk and not be faint" (Isaiah 40:31 NIV).

Maybe life is less about being safe and good, and more about finding God in the space. Maybe life is more about taking the bad and then soaring like eagles anyway. Maybe life is about surrendering control to a good and loving God, accepting hardships as a pathway to peace, and challenges as the means to strength. By faith we trust God with our life and our death, and the diverse terrain that lies in between.

Questions for Self Reflection:

- When have you felt controlled by something or someone?
- In what roles do you feel most out of control?
- In what roles do you excel at exhibiting self control?
- In what ways are you controlling other people or other things instead of controlling self?
- In what ways would you like to let go and trust God?

Intention Statement:

Dear God, grant me the serenity to accept the things I cannot change, the courage to change the things I can, and the wisdom to know the difference.

Extra Study:

Isaiah 58:6; Romans 8:8-9; 1 John 5:19

twenty-five

Pleased as Punch

"I don't know the key to success, but the key to failure is trying to please everybody."

Bill Cosby

Michelle's Story

Michelle was a bright and beautiful young woman, just starting out in a professional career. In college she had strong ideals of wanting to make a difference using her talents in marketing. She was good at her work, and she loved it. Soon after graduation, she found a job at a major magazine and was thrilled with the exciting opportunity. She was self-confident, and began to receive accolades from her superiors right away. These accolades didn't last, however, and she was left with an arm too short to stroke her own ego. She put in long, varied hours, was the first at the office and the last to leave, but felt like her bosses still wanted more from her. She asked people who had been there longer, "What is expected of me? What do they want? How many hours are considered enough?" and never seemed to get a straight answer. She constantly asked her superiors and peers if they thought she was meeting expectations. They gave her good reviews, but she never felt satisfied. She always thought that she could be doing more or better. Her confidence began to wane.

Michelle had not developed a performance shut-off valve. She didn't know how to self-regulate her feelings or expectations. Michelle's mood was triggered by what other people thought about her performance. She worked herself hard for a superior's "atta girl" and when she got it, she experienced her mood alter. All of a sudden, all the exhaustion was worth it because she would get a high. But the highs came further and further apart—and in the interim, she felt depressed. She kept feeling like she was missing the mark, because, after all, pleasing people is a moving target.

Michelle knew where this cycle started. She reported that her dad was a workaholic and was rarely around while she was growing up. The little attention she did get from him was usually instruction on how to do better at school or her chores. In the relational void, these directives were what she thought of as love. She made sense of it like this: to get love and attention, I must perform perfectly. When I do not receive attention, it means that I didn't do well enough to earn it. Her father's emotional withdrawal felt like personal rejection. This caused Michelle a lot of anxiety as an adult.

Michelle was a people-pleaser, and thrived off positive attention. Her task towards maturity was to learn how to regulate her own sense of what was "good enough" instead of trying to please a disapproving god-figure of the past. She,

like all of us, needed to find her "ok-ness" in the consistent unconditional love of God.

Pia Melody, an expert on alcoholism and co-dependency puts it this way, "Your 'bottle' is your desire for unconditional positive regard from another person. Your acknowledgment that you probably aren't going to get consistent unconditional positive regard from anyone parallels the alcoholic's acknowledgment that the bottle isn't really going to make him or her feel better over the long haul." [23] This acknowledgement is an important first step in looking to God for your value and worth instead of people.

Among the people that we want to please the most, are the Lover, the Parents, the Boss, and the Children. We have all tipped our hats to people-pleasing from time to time—especially to avoid trouble with these important figures. Pleasers often think of themselves as being very nice folks, but people pleasing is not a nice thing to do at all. It is a very self-centered activity, motivated by a desire to keep the self elevated to a safe "saintly" status to prevent rejection or abandonment. The pleaser scarcely has a moment to interface with the One True God of love—the One who gives her unconditional, warm, positive regard even when she's *not* being nice.

If you did not receive unconditional love from your god-figures, you can learn to trust God for this need. You can understand that your good deeds and hard work don't earn you a higher approval rating, but that God's love for you is

23 Mellody, Pia. *Facing Love Addiction: Giving yourself the power to change the way you love.* New York, NY: Harper One, 2003.

unchanging and constant. God has already chosen you and will not un-choose you. Your god-figures of the past may have withheld love, acceptance and approval, but God died to give them to you.

Questions for Self Reflection:

- Who are the people in your life that are important to please?
- How much of yourself have you given away to please these people?
- What part of yourself have you had to deny or hide in order to please others?
- In what areas can you accept God's unconditional love in place of trying to please people?

Intention Statement:

God approves of me as His loved and cherished child. I will do my best in response to God's transforming power in my life, not for the approval of other people.

Extra Study:

Acts 4:19; Acts 5:29; Romans 2:13

God
Unwrapped

twenty-six
Desperate to Depend

"He will my shield and portion be, as long as life endures."

John Newton

There is a black, hairy beast that resides in my home. He sleeps on my couch and sneaks food out of my pantry. He was a death-row dog, rescued at the midnight hour and kept in the garage of a friend of a friend of a friend until a new home could be found. As a gesture of good will, I visited the dog that narrowly escaped death with a prepared, "thanks, but no thanks," and was faced with a life altering event. That hairy black "gesture" jumped uninvited into the back of my jeep, and into my heart, and the rest is history.

Frisco is a 105-pound black lab mix with brown eyes like melted chocolate, and an alpha streak that has earned him the nickname "Cujo". Frisco is what you might call, "reactive". Experts say that being reactive is different than being aggressive. Frisco is more of a frightened dog than he is an aggressive dog, but when he feels frightened, he reacts aggressively. Who knows what his history is—he was found on the street without a collar, leading a few other dogs "down the wrong path" and probably was accustomed to defending his alpha role. Well, he met his match.

Since that time, I have learned to be firm and confident with Frisco. The more confident I am, the more secure he is. His tail wags, his ears relax, and he becomes playful. He feels confident that I'm in charge, so he doesn't have to be on guard. He depends on me to make him feel ok.

Unhealthy Reactions to Fear

Being frightened, anxious and insecure is a hallmark to being human. On our own, we just can't shake the intense worries and fears that ail us. Whether it's the anxiety of being lonely, feeling unworthy, unloved, undesirable, inadequate or insignificant, we all have anxious feelings, and we react out of those fears. We, like Frisco, become reactive in response to our fears and choose ways of coping that can often become self-destructive. Many times we've learned coping mechanisms in childhood that helped us adapt and survive in our unhealthy family environment that we must unlearn and replace to have a healthy adulthood. These unhealthy coping mechanisms usually come in the form of dependence on things, people, or forces other than God.

When a person is dependent, it means that she has a pathological relationship with a mood-altering substance or stimulus. The dependent person's relationship with that substance or stimulus becomes more important than real relationships with themselves and other people. This pathological relationship progresses to the point that the stimulus or substance is needed to feel "normal".[24] The mood altering substance or stimulus can be almost anything; food, prescription drugs, pornography, sex, alcohol, risk, control, anger, another person—anything. Here are some common examples:

- The woman who feels insecure and unattractive flirts frequently with men at work, and is dangerously close to indiscretion.
- The man who feels undesirable stays up late on the Internet watching women who know how to communicate "I want you."
- The woman who fears rejection and abandonment works round the clock at making people happy with her so she won't be left alone.
- The man who had to be too responsible too early in life has a mid-life crisis where he shirks adult responsibilities and others' expectations.
- The woman who feels unloved and lonely comforts herself with fatty and salty foods.
- The man who feels lonely and disconnected creates adrenaline pumping thrills and risk taking highs to feel alive.

These compulsive behaviors alter our moods, and keep us coming back to them to feel relief from pain and anxiety. Though seemingly benign at first, they are increasingly

24 Carnes, Patrick. *Out of the Shadows: Understanding Sexual Addiction.* Center City, Minnesota: Hazeldon, 2001, p. 14-16.

difficult to stop, and result in putting a wedge between us and God.

In our own way, we all have experienced misplaced dependencies. Dependencies come in all shapes and sizes, and require more and more of our lives, time, mental energy, and resources to bring about the same feeling of "ok-ness". Dr. Patrick Carnes says that when we begin to live in sincere delusion, believing our own lies, our dependency turns into addiction. If you find yourself in the middle of an unhealthy dependency and you've started to hide it, you may be on your way to addiction. You may even try to justify your pathological dependency with arguments, rationalizing, excuses, blame shifting, and flat-out denial.

Getting Free from Dependencies

Traditionally, the first step to recovery is admitting that we are powerless over our fears and our unhealthy ways to cope, and that we can't get free of them on our own. We must be willing to say to ourselves, "What I've been trying is not working. God's approach to life is the only way that really works." Carnes says, "Generally, addicts do not perceive themselves as worthwhile persons. Nor do they believe that other people would care for them or meet their needs if everything was known about them, including the addiction."[25] That is precisely why getting help from other trusted people is so necessary.

In order to heal, we must face the pain or rebellion that caused us to act out in the first place. The demons that we bring out of the dark wither in the light. The giant that we run

---

25 Carnes, Patrick. *Out of the Shadows: Understanding Sexual Addiction.* Center City, Minnesota: Hazeldon, 2001, p. 14-16.

to meet is the one that we defeat. Pain is part of the growing process, but suffering doesn't have to be.

Sitting *with* the pain and discomfort is different than sitting *in* it. Sitting in it means that you take the time and attention you need to identify the problem, address it, and explore the affect it has on you. It also means forgiving it, and letting it go. This is a process. God has your healing and restoration in mind when you trust Him with your needs. This happens through turning to God, moment by moment, in the face of temptation. This happens in your alone time with God and in groups of supportive people who accept you in spite of your troubles. This happens as you gain more power and control in your life and develop a solid sense of self. These things take time and effort, without a doubt. But there is no other way to live.

The Bible says,

> And that means killing off everything connected with that way of death: sexual promiscuity, impurity, lust, doing whatever you feel like whenever you feel like it, and grabbing whatever attracts your fancy. That's a life shaped by things and feelings instead of by God. It's because of this kind of thing that God is about to explode in anger. It wasn't long ago that you were doing all that stuff and not knowing any better. But you know better now, so make sure it's all gone for good: bad temper, irritability, meanness, profanity, dirty talk.
>
> So, chosen by God for this new life of love, dress in

> the wardrobe God picked out for you: compassion, kindness, humility, quiet strength, discipline. Be even-tempered, content with second place, quick to forgive an offense. Forgive as quickly and completely as the Master forgave you. And regardless of what else you put on, wear love. It's your basic, all-purpose garment. Never be without it.
>
> Colossians 3:5-14 MSG

God's finger isn't wagging at us because of our misbehaviors. Rather, His arms are open to us saying, "Leave death behind, and get love instead." God says that there is a new way of living—a way that exchanges our unhealthy dependencies on things, people, and substances, for a love relationship with God. Depending on a dependable God means that we never have to act out of fear and insecurity, because the firm love of our God is in control of our lives and He can be trusted to take care of us.

Frisco still gets ruffled from time to time around other dogs that he distrusts, but he looks at me first before he lunges for attack. I usually give him a quick tug on his collar to let him know that I'm still in charge, and he can depend on me to keep him safe. Now, to get him to stop counter surfing…

Questions for Self Reflection:

- What unhealthy dependencies have you had in the past or present?
- What pain or fear has propelled you toward these dependencies?
- What childhood coping mechanisms helped you to survive then, but need to be surrendered now?
- Instead of depending on stimulus and substances to make you feel ok, how would you like to invite God into your weaknesses?
- What are some ways that you can clothe yourself in love? For yourself? For others?
- If you are planning to leave unhealthy dependencies behind, what does "love" look like in place of them? How can love be manifested in your life, instead of dependency?

Intention Statement:

Day by day, moment by moment, I will depend on God to live a life of love and liberty. I don't have to do this on my own, and I don't have to do it the way I've always done. With God's help, I can wear "love" for Him, myself and for others.

Extra Study:

2 Corinthians 6:18; 2 Corinthians 5:9- 6:8; Ephesians 5:3; Ephesians 5:5; Hebrew 12:16

God
Unwrapped

twenty-seven

The Crotchety Old Neighbor

"My son, do not despise the LORD's discipline and do not resent his rebuke, because the LORD disciplines those he loves, as a father the son he delights in."

Proverbs 3:11-12 NIV

One day I was talking to a friend about an "issue" I was having. I had talked to her about this before and she thoughtfully responded, "It sounds like this keeps cycling back for you." She was right. This "issue" was no stranger and it was draining my energy.

My problem was like an old crotchety neighbor who kept coming for unwelcomed visits, and begrudgingly, I kept opening the door to her. All of a sudden she would be in my living room, eating my fancy crackers, drinking my good wine, telling me the things I should be doing, and taking up all my time. When she visited, I felt small and judged, and uncertain. I felt like I needed the old neighbor to "keep me in line," and to "keep me from the wicked desires of my heart," and to "make sure I wasn't getting too uppity." I needed her to remind me of all the things I was forgetting to worry about.

Issues of guilt, self doubt, festering anger, control, bitterness, and fear are things that drain our energy and steal our peace. God desires to cut these things out of our lives because they strangle our growth. Ole Crotchety had a stranglehold on my heart, and I knew I needed God's help.

God's Green Thumb and What Jesus Has to Say About It

One day, probably while walking past a vineyard, Jesus used the common vine to tell of the uncommon life He could offer. He told His disciples that He was the True Vine, and His Father was the vinedresser. Jesus drew His life from God who nurtured, maintained, and supported Him. Jesus likened His disciples to branches that grew out of the vine. He said, "Yes, I am the vine; you are the branches. Those who remain in me, and I in them, will produce much fruit. For apart from me you can do nothing" (John 15:5 NLT).

When Ole Crotchety was around, bitter fruit was my only produce. I wondered what Jesus meant by "Those who remain in me, and I in them, will produce much fruit." What does *remaining* look like? Imagine a vine supported by an anchor and deeply rooted in the ground and growing upward and outward. Jesus is that vine. God provides the anchor, the water, the care, and everything the vine needs to thrive. Also, imagine the vine producing branches from its core—branches that bud and flower and produce fruit. The branches are nothing without the vine. We depend on Jesus, as Jesus depends on the Father. This is the picture that Jesus gave to His disciples on how to live the good life. We are

connected to the Divine: we live in Him and out of Him and He lives in us. We receive our life from Jesus.

As part of His disciplinary role, the Father prunes dead, diseased, and non-producing branches. Any good gardener knows that pruning is just as important as fertilizing and nurturing. God, as the Master Vine Dresser knows how, when, and where to cut to make the healthiest, fruit-producing branches. As we submit to His discipline, He cuts out the activities, patterns, and relationships that drain us and make us sick.

In my case, I was abiding with the familiar, yet unpleasable Ole Crotchety, and not in Christ. God cut out the dead thing that was sucking the energy from the rest of me, and for a while, I had to get used to a quiet house. Since Ole Crotchety wasn't around telling me what to do, I had to learn to hear God's voice in the stillness. Like the winter after the pruning, the quiet was just uncomfortable enough that I was tempted to invite my old neighbor back. This is the point that growth doesn't feel like growth—it's slow, lonely and quiet, but it is loving. In the stillness, I learned about God's love, and the ways of love. In the absence of the old, the new has a chance to grow. I invited God into my house, and we rekindled a dialog that awakened my dreams and passions and peace. He brought His own crackers (unleavened) and I felt glad to be back in His company. Jesus says, "As the Father loved Me, I also have loved you; abide in My love" (John 15:9 NKJV). During that season, I didn't know a lot, but in comparison to my new companion, I knew that Ole Crotchety was not love.

Jesus told His disciples, "You have already been pruned and purified by the message I have given you. Remain in me, and I will remain in you" (John 15:3-4 NLT). We already have been given a new identity, and we are in Christ as branches are in the Vine, so the work of "being good enough" is done. We depend on Jesus for everything in life. *Our growth occurs out of this dependence.* The branch doesn't have to strain to produce fruit. The fruit just happens. Ever seen a grape try to grow? No, it just grows as it remains connected to the vine. The branch doesn't have to do anything but depend on the Vine to produce good things. To depend on anything else, cuts us off from life.

Jesus says, "When you obey my commandments, you remain in my love, just as I obey my Father's commandments and remain in his love. I have told you these things so that you will be filled with my joy. Yes, your joy will overflow! This is my commandment: Love each other in the same way I have loved you" (John 15:10-12 NLT). God's ways are always about love. Following these ways produces the fruit of joy in us, and then we are able to infect the people around us. When we are living and abiding in this love we are drinking from the well often, accepting love for ourselves because we need it, not because we earned it, and giving love to others without condition.

Questions for Self Reflection:

- What does abiding in Christ feel like for you?
- How can you tell the difference between abiding in the Vine and being apart from the Vine?
- Do you have activities, patterns, or relationships that get in the way of you remaining in Christ?
- In what areas would you like to submit to God's pruning in your life?
- Have you experienced a time of God's pruning? Can you relate to a "winter" after the pruning? What kind of fruit was produced after the pruning?

Intention Statement:

My only job is to depend on God for everything I need. He will show me, provide for me, and sustain me. I move, and breathe, and have my being in Christ.

Extra Study:

Job 5:17; Proverbs 3:11; Proverbs 3:12; Proverbs 6:23; 2 Timothy 1:7; Hebrew 12:10

God
Unwrapped

twenty-eight
Mission Possible

"There is no passion to be found playing small—in settling for a life that is less than the one you are capable of living."

Nelson Mandela

When I talk to kids in my office, we inevitably address foul treatment from other kids at school. Kids can't always prevent sour pusses, bullies, and queen bees from picking on them, but they can be confident in the face of playground and locker room torture. Something my young clients repeat in my office is, "I am not for picking on," or "I am for respect!" Some will feel the truth of the statements so strongly, that they just have to shout them out. I've learned the hard way that it's best to meet these kids after hours, so there's no chance of disturbing the neighbors.

We make it less about the offender and more about the child's sense of self. Being reminded of the truth of who they are and their inherent value gives them the confidence they need to take the appropriate steps at school, whatever those steps may be.

Jesus had this kind of confidence. He knew who He was in the face of temptation, popular adoration, and governmental oppression. To anyone watching, at the time of His crucifixion, Christ's death would have looked like a pointless waste of a promising life, but Jesus knew who He was, and what He was meant to do. His identity was fixed and firm. What would happen if we had this same sense of "knowing?"

I think Rosa Parks did.

On December 1st, 1955, in Montgomery, Alabama, Rosa Parks refused to give up her seat on the city bus for a white man, which she was required by law to do. She was arrested on that same day and later found guilty. Just less than a year later, in November of 1956, segregation on Montgomery buses was declared unconstitutional by the United States Supreme Court. Her quiet, courageous act changed America, its view of the value of African Americans, and redirected the course of history. Acts like this influenced thousands of people, including Martin Luther King, Jr., to rally together to peacefully protest and demand equal rights for all.

Rosa was quoted as saying, "I will no longer act on the outside in a way that contradicts the truth that I hold deeply inside. I will no longer act as if I were less than the whole person I know myself to be." It was her sense of self-worth and inherent value that strengthened her resolve against injustice. It was Jesus knowing His true identity that enabled Him to endure suffering for our sake. We must know who we really are before we can fully embark into God's mission for our lives.

The Whole Person

The word *integrity* comes from the Latin *integer*, meaning a whole number, not a fraction. When someone lacks integrity, they experience goal conflict, self- and God-doubt, and what the Bible describes as being "double minded." James says, "But let him ask in faith, with no doubting, for he who doubts is like a wave of the sea driven and tossed by the wind. For let not that man suppose that he will receive anything from the Lord; he is a double-minded man, unstable in all his ways" (James 1:6-8 NKJV). He doesn't know who he really is, who he wants to be, or who he wants to please. A "fractioned" person cannot have kingdom impact because his beliefs and purposes are in conflict.

Integrity is much more than being honest or abiding by ethics. Integrity has to do with the core of a person. William Backus, author of *Telling Each Other the Truth* describes integrity this way: "it stands for manifesting in life and words the truth a person knows and possesses in his heart. When he knows the truth about what he is within and then allows that truth to surface, he has integrity."

Rosa Parks believed herself to be a whole person of equal worth and stature to her white peers, and decided on December 1st, 1955 to courageously start living that way on the outside. She did so with some real cost to herself, but ultimately it was a great gain for society. What obstacles do you need to overcome before you are a whole person? What ghosts from the past, stereotypes of the present, or religious rules keep you fractioned off from who God meant you to be?

Jesus anchored His identity in His ongoing relationship with His Father God. He called him "Daddy" and God called Jesus, "beloved Son." Jesus stole away in the middle of the night to be alone with Him, nurturing His love relationship with God. This love relationship solidified Jesus' view of Himself as treasured and loved with a mission to seek and save the lost, even in the face of public disdain, the betrayal of a friend, and ultimate torture on a cross. Jesus could pursue and complete the mission because He knew who He was. Even up to the last, He had the chance to save His own life by denying who He was when Pilot asked Him, "Are you the king of the Jews?" Jesus replied, "Yes, it is as you say" (Matthew 27:11 NIV), because He was a man of integrity and would not compromise who He knew himself to be, no matter the cost. Where would we be if He had denied the fullness of His identity? Where will you be, if you do?

Anna's Story

Anna was a 30-something woman who had felt the calling to become a medical surgeon. She was a wife and a mother and feared how this career would impact her family. She began to pursue her desire and scheduled time to study for the arduous MCAT exam to be admitted into medical school. She came to me with the question, "Should I pursue this dream to be a doctor, or should I be a stay-at-home mom and home school?"

I noticed that there was a Grand Canyon divide between the two options and asked, "Wow, that seems like a pretty big either/or."

She said, "Well, it's like I am in a lose-lose situation. I feel bad when I spend time with my son, because I am not studying, and I feel bad when I am studying because I am not with my son."

"Well, could there be a both/and instead?"

Anna had a history of denying her God-given voice to please the people around her. Anna's parents were very much into their own activities, jobs, and friends without giving much time or attention to their children. To garner the attention that Anna needed, she became very astute at predicting and meeting her parents' needs. She learned early on to deny her own desires, interests, and needs in order to be close to her parents. At one point, Anna was sexually abused by some older children, and her family's response to the abuse was virtually no response at all, thereby reinforcing her insignificance.

Because children by nature are self-centered, they direct any parental dysfunction back onto themselves. Since a child's parents are her only lifeline to security and provision, it is too overwhelming to believe that her parents are not able to provide her what she needs, so she believes that she is the one with the problem. Anna made sense of her family's neglect this way: "If I just do better, or try harder, then they will start to care." She denied the truth of her own feelings and her own worth so she could believe the best about her parents.

As an adult, Anna had to listen to the God-given voice of her own value and give attention to the desires of her heart, instead of quieting them to please her family. Once she began

to give the desires of her heart a voice and a function, she felt the tension of the possibility of not being pleasing enough, good enough, and quiet-natured enough. She had to learn that her voice was important and worth hearing, and that most of the guilt she experienced for having desire was just the old way of keeping her quiet. Once healed from the past, she was able to identify and validate her desires without guilt. Anna was beginning to understand herself as a worthwhile person with inherent value. She changed her identity from victim to overcomer.

One day, while in my office, I asked Anna to describe what being a doctor meant to her, and why she desired it. Her body relaxed, her eyes went up as if fetching a dream out of the sky, and she smiled. "I love to study biochemistry and organic chemistry because I get to see the art behind the science." Her face was peaceful. "I get to see God as a Great Master of art." I felt God himself in the room at that moment. To deny that part of herself would be to deny God's purpose for her life, and the scientific nature of the Spirit within her. It would be Anna getting up from her seat and standing at the back of the bus, denying who she really was on the inside.

Anna will be tempted to follow others' expectations of her. She will be faced with decisions regarding her son's care and hours that seem impossible. But as she knows herself to be a whole and valuable person, alive with purpose and passion, she will fulfill the call of God in her life in ways she never expected.

If you know who you are in Christ, you will accomplish great things.

Questions for Self Reflection:

- Are there parts of yourself that you hide or deny so that you can be acceptable or pleasing to others?
- What parts of your life do you want to bring into wholeness, acting the same way on the outside as you feel on the inside?
- What goals and dreams do you have for yourself?
- How have you been tempted to deny that calling in order to play it safe?
- What fears or doubts keep you from pursuing God's calling on your life?
- How can you surrender those fears and doubts to God and step out in obedience?

Intention Statement:

I will no longer act on the outside in a way that contradicts the truth that I hold deeply inside. I will no longer act as if I were less than the whole person I know myself to be.

Extra Study:

1 Corinthians 13:11-12; Mark 11:22-24; Luke 23:38; Matthew 21:21; John 17:7

twenty-nine

Flying

"You know how I carried you on eagles' wings and brought you to myself."

Exodus 19:4-6 NLT

One of the many perks of living in the Pacific Northwest is the frequent sightings of bald eagles. No matter how many I see, I am still fascinated with their majesty. I was walking in downtown Seattle one afternoon and was surprised to see one flying between the sky scrapers so close that if I leaped, I could have plucked his tail feather.

Frances Hammerstrom, an animal conservationist, recorded her observations of big birds in many books. In her book *An Eagle to Sky*, she writes the story of an eaglet perched in a nest, too old to be babied, and too scared to fly.

> The.....eaglet was now alone in the nest. Each time a parent came flying in toward the nest he called for food eagerly; but over and over again, [the parent] came with empty feet, and the eaglet grew thinner. He pulled meat scraps from the old dried-up carcasses

lying around the nest. He watched a sluggish carrion beetle, picked it up gingerly, and ate it. His first kill.

Days passed, and as he lost body fat he became quicker in his movements and paddled ever more lightly when the wind blew, scarcely touching the nest edge; from time to time he was airborne for a moment or two.

Parents often flew past and sometimes fed him. Beating his wings and teetering on the edge of the nest, he screamed for food whenever one flew by. And a parent often flew past just out of reach, carrying delectable meals: a half-grown jack rabbit or a plump rat raided from a dump. Although he was hungry almost all the time, he was becoming more playful as he lost his baby fat; sometimes, when no parent bird was in sight, he pounced ferociously on a scrap of prairie dog skin or on old bits of dried bone.

The male eaglet stayed by himself for the most part. He was no longer brooded at night. Hunger and the cold mountain nights were having their effect, not only on his body but on his disposition. A late frost hit the valley, and a night wind ruffled his feathers and chilled his body. When the sunlight reached the eyrie's (the brood in a nest of a bird of prey) edge, he sought its warmth; and soon, again, he was bounding in the wind, now light and firm-muscled.

A parent flew by, downwind, dangling a young marmot in its feet. The eaglet almost lost his balance in his eagerness for food. Then the parent swung by

> again, closer, upwind, and riding the updraft by the eyrie, as though daring him to fly. Lifted light by the wind, he was airborne, flying—or more gliding—for the first time in his life. He sailed across the valley to make a scrambling, almost tumbling landing on a bare knoll. As he turned to get his bearings the parent dropped the young marmot nearby. Half running, half flying he pounced on it, mantled, and ate his fill.[26]

Hammerstrom's observations could easily be the observations of a social psychologist looking in on parents with their young adult child, a pastor and his intern, or a senior doctor and her residents. We experience the feelings of this young eaglet when we no longer need to be spoon fed and coddled. There was a time for this, of course—a time that we needed healing and comfort, care and provision. But for God to do this for us for very long would be demoralizing. It would keep us children forever. He wants us to grow, to mature and to thrive as active adults—to take our place in the sky.

Why do we stay in the nest picking at dry bones and beetles? Why do we let the confines of the old ways keep us from experiencing what we were born to do? God wants us to be like Him, to follow in His footsteps and to soar in His current. We are afraid that our wings won't hold us, but hasn't God already provided what we needed to be strong? If we were not strong enough to fly, then we wouldn't have the insatiable urge to do it. It is this urge that tells us we are ready.

---

26 Hammerstrom, Frances. *An Eagle to the Sky*. Guilford, CT: Lyons Press, 1970.

We are afraid that we will be on our own, all alone, plummeting to our doom. But hasn't God already promised to catch us when we fall? And isn't it true that every raptor must feel the inertia of falling before he knows how to fly out of it?

We are afraid that we do not have what it takes to support ourselves. But hasn't our Father been teaching us since the day we were born? Hasn't He been modeling to us what is needed? Hasn't he given us opportunities to practice along the way? Doesn't He know what we need even before we ask it? Much like the eaglet parent in Hammerstrom's story, He waits for us to feel our wings, and our strength, and the exhilaration and pride of the flight before He swoops in to take care of our needs. He is not only about mothering us, which is good and right in its time, He is also about empowering us. By His power, we will grow into the people He destined us to be.

God says, "Now if you will obey me and keep my covenant, you will be my own special treasure from among all the peoples on earth; for all the earth belongs to me. And you will be my kingdom of priests, my holy nation" (Exodus 19:5-6 NLT). What do priests do? They bring people to God. They point to God. And they are pictures of God.

As we live in our new identity, we become aware of our purpose. God says of us, "I have made you a light to the Gentiles, to bring salvation to the farthest corners of the earth" (Acts 13:47 NLT). We are the light of the world, and a city on a hill. We are the salt of the earth, preserving humanity for the prospect of redemption through Christ. (Matthew 5:13-16). We bring good news to people—the same freedom

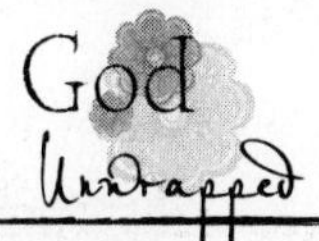

that we have experienced is available to everyone. And we don't just talk about this freedom, we live it out, giving grace and love to those we have contact with. This is us, healed and transformed, free to be who God has created us to be, soaring in the strength of Christ, and living a life of grace. It is infectious.

"How beautiful on the mountains are the feet of the messenger who brings good news, the good news of peace and salvation, the news that the God of Israel reigns!" (Isaiah 52:7 NLT).

Questions for Self Reflection:

- What is God asking of you right now that feels scary or uncertain?
- What keeps you from leaving the nest and learning to fly?
- What has happened in the past when you tried something new?
- Have you experienced the exhilaration and pride of flying before? Have you crash landed? How did you experience God in those times?

Intention Statement:

I will step out of my safety zone, and trust God to fulfill His purpose in me. Only God knows my fullest potential, and I trust Him to lead me to fulfill it.

Extra Study:

John 6:5-13; Luke 17:5-10; Mark 4:40;
Mark 5:34; Mark 10:52

thirty

Give It Away

"Today I appoint you to stand up..."

Jeremiah 1:10 NLT

Time stopped on this crisp and frosty winter morning. If you were looking at a freeze frame, you would have seen my hundred pound dog lifting his leg, relieving himself on my neighbor's pants and shoe, steam rising, shock and horror etched on my face, and me, helpless to stop the canine infraction from taking place. My grandfatherly neighbor was headed to a funeral. Before he left for the day, he decided to take his dogs for a quick romp around the open school yard, where my dog, Frisco, and I were playing fetch. I was relaying my condolences for his loss when I noticed Frisco's insolence, and was shocked into inaction until the deed was done. The awful thing was that my neighbor didn't notice. He kept talking while the steam rose and his pant leg dripped, not knowing he had just been marked as Frisco's territory. Then I was faced with the terrible dilemma, "Do I tell him the truth?" Telling him would certainly be awkward and embarrassing for both of us, but I couldn't let him go to a funeral that way. He had to know the truth, no matter how painful, awkward, embarrassing, or friendship-sabotaging it may be. I yelled at Frisco, that being the least I could do, and then humbly mumbled something about "I'm so sorry," and "my dog just...," and "yeah, I'll let you go change your clothes while I go hide until spring."

God's purpose is for us to know the truth about Him, and for us to tell other people too. Lucky for us, it's a lot better news to tell than the news I had to give to my neighbor. In fact, sharing the gospel of Jesus with other people just means that we are sharing the "good news" with them. When we tell the truth of God to others, we are offering them freedom.

God's purpose for our lives is greater than we ever imagined for ourselves—with a wider scope and depth of influence. As we surrender to God's working in our lives, we also surrender to His greater purpose for our lives in the world. Our call is not only to know God for ourselves, but it is also to make Him known to others.

I have a friend, Nancy, who desired to have a healed relationship with her mother for a long time. That relationship was emotionally tense, awkward, and often obligatory. My friend discussed her concerns with her mom, set healthy boundaries and even invited a mediator to help them work things out. The mediator took my friend aside and told her that it was time to forgive her mother. She said, "I don't mean forgive and pretend that everything is fine. I mean stop holding her accountable for the past." This really rattled Nancy. She really didn't want to forgive her mom until her mom took responsibility for her part of the relationship. She was mad at the mediator. She wanted to fire her. Instead, Nancy left the meeting and did some soul searching. She knew the mediator was right. She gave up trying to "fix" the relationship, and started investigating what "forgiveness" really looked like.

On the phone one day, she said to me, "I need to forgive my mom." Now, she's not the kind to just sit on a proclamation like that. Nancy's the kind to hunt it down and kill it! Less than two weeks later, my friend called me and told me of a series of extraordinary events that lead her to not only forgiveness, but freedom. This person met that person, and coincidentally, that person had just been to a seminar, and this other person was praying, and then she remembered a childhood memory and the person who went to the seminar knew what to do with that memory, and then crying in a parking lot, she let go and was filled with compassion for her mom…and on and on.

And forgiveness overwhelmed her.

Because the mediator spoke the truth to her about the powerful, empowering act of forgiveness, a string of spiritual activity began on Nancy's behalf.

Motivated to Share

One day as Jesus was traveling from His hometown to another, He saw a tax collector named Matthew, working in his booth. "Jesus said to him, 'Follow me,' and he stood up and followed Jesus" (Matthew 9:9 NCV). After meeting Jesus,

Matthew wanted to introduce Him to the people around him. Jesus ate at Matthew's house and all of Matthew's friends and business associates came to meet Him.

Sharing the truth about God with other people, whether overtly or by life example, is the same as introducing them to Christ. The work of the Holy Spirit in our lives causes us to love like Jesus loves, and it reveals to others Who God really is. To live out the lives that we are currently living in a way that is loving and true, is our highest call. God brings people into our sphere of influence to experience this love and truth. And then we point to the Father, like Jesus pointed to the Father, so that the people around us can experience what we have.

The Bible makes some claims about what will happen when we obey God in living out this kind of life. God says, "Look, I have put my words in your mouth! Today I appoint you to stand up against nations and kingdoms. Some you must uproot and tear down, destroy and overthrow. Others you must build up and plant" (Jeremiah 1:9-10 NLT).

Spiritually speaking, God appoints us to stand up against the worldly kingdoms that represent the patterns of the world's ways, which are counter to God's ways. He calls us to uproot and tear down the things that are unjust, unrighteous, and unloving, so that His kingdom of peace and joy and abundance can rule. He appoints us to overthrow the strongholds of power that keep slavery in place and freedom at bay. Spiritually speaking, these things start in our own hearts, and are often a part of a parallel process as we influence others to do the same. As we walk as liberated people, it inspires and empowers others to experience liberation too. When we've experienced God's love, we just have to give it away.

Paul's letter to the Romans says, "Therefore, I urge you, brothers, in view of God's mercy, to offer your bodies as living sacrifices, holy and pleasing to God—this is your spiritual act of worship. Do not conform any longer to the pattern of this world, but be transformed by the renewing of your mind. Then you will be able to test and approve what God's will is—his good, pleasing and perfect will" (Romans 12:1-2 NIV).

God not only appoints us to this calling, He provides all that we need to accomplish the calling. To feel like this calling is a burden means that *we* are feeling responsible to see it through. To feel like this calling is a duty means that we have, in an instant, departed from God's abiding love and set to work on our own.

However, to feel like this calling is an *opportunity*, is to be joined with God in the work. To feel like this calling is an *adventure*, is to be cooperating with God, walking with Him and happily depending on Him to see His own work accomplished. We are able to see others in the bondage we once experienced, and want to bring freedom to them too. This is how God intends for us to feel about our calling. Then we can be the hands and feet of Jesus to a dying and desperate world.

Questions for Self Reflection:

- How do you see your calling as a benefit to those around you and around the world?
- List the people and things you care most deeply about (ranging from your family to nations and organizations). How can you impact them with the love and liberty of Christ that you've experienced?
- How has knowing Christ changed you, and how would you like to see Christ change others?
- What characteristic of God's do you want people to know about the most?
- What message have you been uniquely equipped to give and live out to others?

Intention Statement:

I will know God, and I will make Him known. I am becoming the person God intended me to be.

Extra Study:

Isaiah 52:6-8; 2 Corinthians 9:10-15; Psalms 119:30

thirty-one
The More Excellent Way

"If you are going to achieve excellence in big things, you develop the habit in little matters. Excellence is not an exception, it is a prevailing attitude."

General Colin Powell

There are natural hazards to living where "the sun don't shine": gloominess, grumpiness, sogginess and low vitamin D levels. Seattle gets around 226 cloudy days a year, with most of those days including some sort of precipitation. But, Lord, when the sun shines here, it is heaven on earth! Snow-peaked mountains, sea gulls and fishing boats, tulips blooming, fish flying in the market, coffee flowing, music ringing, heavily tattooed people grinning from ear to ear—ahh, there's no place like Seattle in the sunshine! It is simply amazing what a little light can bring to a dark place.

You are that light. You are a gift to the world around you. The people in your world are lucky and blessed to have you. It's possible that they've forgotten because maybe you've been overcast lately, so shine your light to remind them again.

Jesus tells a story of a boss going on a business trip and leaving his property and business to be overseen by his employees. To the first employee, he gives $5000 to invest and steward until his return. To the second employee, he gives $2000 to invest and steward, and to the third, he gives $1000, all according to their individual abilities. Like any good boss, he is expecting that the employees will do something good with the money—something that adds to the overall bottom line of the business, while keeping in line with the company values and goals.

The first employees do not disappoint, and in fact have doubled their investments by the time the boss gets back. The boss is so pleased that he rewards them with promotions to the level of partner. Oh, but the third bloke is toast. He doesn't do anything with the money. He doesn't let it earn interest, give it to the poor, or even buy a Louis Vuitton wallet. He buries it in the dirt. Employee #3 believes that the boss is harsh and exacting and has little tolerance for failure, so he is afraid to lose the money. The boss gets mad that the employee wasted the great opportunity and is furious at the employee's unfounded assumptions and fears. He takes the $1000 and gives it to the employee who took the most risk, and fires #3.

Your opportunity to make a difference awaits you. God gives you the means to do it, and then lets you decide how you will make it happen. Whether in entrepreneurial pursuits, business management, ministry, social justice, community activism, relationship renovation, medical advancements, world-wide missions, or neighborhood missions, ask God for your opportunity. Ask Him for your next capital venture, your next big idea, or your next light bulb moment. He wants to give it to you. He just wants you to ask. Here are a few things to consider.

Identify Your Dark World: Where do you live and where is it gloomiest? What is the felt need of the people around you? Who is your target market? What would make their lives better? Who are you naturally inclined to shine on? What kind of person is drawn to you? Within what context are you practicing, working, living, and raising your family?

Identify Your Currency: If God has given you the ability to invest, what is your currency? What has He given you to make a difference in the world? What are your strengths? Look beyond your resume bullet points and identify your personality strengths that meet the felt need. How do you relate to other people? How do you get things done? Do you lead or support? What do you have that your world needs?

Identify Your Interest: What are you passionate about? Who do you care about? What do you care about? What do you want to be the very best at? What gets your motor revving? What stimulates and invigorates you? What gets you mad and motivated to do something about it?

Make a Goal: Did employees #1 and #2 dream on a small scale? Did they just *hope* for their money to double? Did they think like employees or did they think like partners? Dream a dream, and make a goal. God is in the dream—don't worry about that. What is your vision for yourself, your family, your career, or your community? What is your vision for your world? After you make the goal, make your sub-goals to see where you're at, where you want to be, and how you want to get there. Don't tell yourself it's not possible.

Take Risks: I don't mean be risky. Do your due diligence, plan, learn, save, and then flex your faith muscle and fly. Take progressive, incremental risks toward and into your passion. Use the talents, gifts, connections, networks, and finances that God has given you and move toward your goal. Make yourself vulnerable, stretch your wings and feel the fear of falling. Fear just makes decisive faith even more decisive.

Do What It Takes to Be Your Best: I've talked a lot about feeling like you're good enough to be accepted, loved and called. But don't just stop at being good enough. Be excellent. Be the best at what you do. Be known for the excellence of your work, your integrity, ingenuity, attention to detail, intuitiveness, and foresight. Invest time and money in learning from the best in your field. Be committed to professional development and personal growth. Look for opportunities to expand your territory and deepen your knowledge.

Fail Forward: Take every disappointment, every fallen stock, every failing grade, every lost job, every rejection letter, and every failed attempt at relationship restoration as a lesson to learn from. Each failure offers more useful information than a whole semester worth of college classes. Recognize that God is in the failures and God is in the successes and God is in the mediocre and mundane. It's more about the *process* than the *product*. God is more interested in the condition, health, and splendor of your soul than what you consider to be success or failure. Success and failure are subject to God's resurrection-type work bringing life out of death, which can

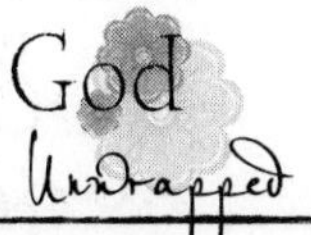

occur many years after you stop paying attention. Your job is to take each of life's events and use them for your ultimate growth and God's ultimate glory.

Every day when my kids leave for school, I say the same thing: "The world is lucky to have you, now go make a difference in it." We have the potential to lead millions in the light and love of God. We have the ability to ignite, spark, and fan the flame in the darkness. The world is blessed to have you—now go make a difference in it.

Questions for Self Reflection:

- Go back and answer the questions listed above about passion, purpose, and audience.
- Answer the questions about felt need and how you are uniquely equipped to meet that need.

Intention Statement:

I know my Father, and I know His light is within me. I choose to let it shine in everything I do, depending fully on God and basking in His daily delight.

Extra Study:

Philippians 2:14-15; 2 Corinthians 8:7; Matthew 25:14-30

We'd Like to Hear from You!

If you found this book to be transformative and would like to give your feedback, please visit God Unwrapped at www.harrisonhouse.com.

If you would like to stay connected, please visit:

www.Godunwrapped.com

for additional discussions and resources. You can also show your support for this project by liking God Unwrapped on Facebook. Thank you in advance for telling your friends about it so they can experience God's love in a new way too.

PRAYER OF SALVATION

God loves you—no matter who you are, no matter what your past. God loves you so much that He gave His one and only begotten Son for you. The Bible tells us that "...whoever believes in him shall not perish but have eternal life" (John 3:16 NIV). Jesus laid down His life and rose again so that we could spend eternity with Him in heaven and experience His absolute best on earth. If you would like to receive Jesus into your life, say the following prayer out loud and mean it from your heart.

Heavenly Father, I come to You admitting that I am a sinner. Right now, I choose to turn away from sin, and I ask You to cleanse me of all unrighteousness. I believe that Your Son, Jesus, died on the cross to take away my sins. I also believe that He rose again from the dead so that I might be forgiven of my sins and made righteous through faith in Him. I call upon the name of Jesus Christ to be the Savior and Lord of my life. Jesus, I choose to follow You and ask that You fill me with the power of the Holy Spirit. I declare that right now I am a child of God. I am free from sin and full of the righteousness of God. I am saved in Jesus' name. Amen.

If you prayed this prayer to receive Jesus Christ as your Savior for the first time, please contact us on the Web at **www.harrisonhouse.com** to receive a free book.

Or you may write to us at

Harrison House • P.O. Box 35035 • Tulsa, Oklahoma 74153

About the Author

Michelle Hollomon is a licensed counselor and certified professional coach with thousands of hours helping people achieve their personal and professional goals. Her unique style of communicating allows her to temper the gravity of serious issues with the hope and humor of a person who's been there and overcome. She works with people from all walks of life, from top level executives and church leaders, to couples and children, helping them realize the life they were destined to live. She has lived internationally, been a military wife, run two successful private practices, climbed 14ers, is raising two sweet and sassy daughters, married to one dashing man, and drives topless in the summer time (top down Jeep Wrangler, that is). Audiences find her style engaging, funny, and extremely applicable to felt needs.